WHAT'S STOPPING YOU TODAY?

Create Your Best Life

6 Keys to Energizing Success

Cynthia Howard RN, CNC, PhD

Copyright © 2019 Cynthia Howard RN, CNC, PhD

ISBN: 978-0-578-44808-4

Cover design by Todd Siatkowsky, Special Forces Art Department

All rights reserved. No part of this book may be reproduced or transmitted in any form or by any means, electronic or mechanical, including photocopying, recording or by any information storage and retrieval system without written permission of the publisher, except for the inclusion of brief quotations in a review.

Printed in the United States of America

www.eileadership.org

This is your guide to being unstoppable.

Go for it.

Note to Readers

How to Use this Book

This book outlines six keys to energize your success. The extremely important second chapter explains the foundation for the program. An online portal accompanies the book, providing additional resources to help you move beyond whatever barriers are blocking your success.

The premise of the book is that your view of *you*—how you think about yourself—matters more than anything. The exercises in this book, as well as online, are designed to uncover mindset habits that get in the way of achieving your goals.

One of the key mindset shifts involves identifying and owning your strengths instead of focusing on your weaknesses. These strengths are your superpowers. You will have access to a premier assessment for strengths called the *Strengths Profile*. This is included in the online program. An introduction to strengths is in Chapter 2, as well as in the online program.

This leads to another mindset shift: managing your energy versus your time. Living in the age of distraction has taken its toll on the ability to focus. Distractions costs time and energy and contributes to irritability. This book includes a self-assessment on the Resilience Pyramid. Go through that assessment and find out which areas in your life might need more attention.

Be sure to join the private Facebook group, where we have discussions and post updated content. Get your questions answered. Be part of the conversations. I look forward to seeing you inside!

CONTENTS

Life Happens: Do You Roll, Bounce, or Get Stuck? 8
  How You See Yourself Matters More Than Anything You Do 10
    6 Keys to Energizing Success 13

Get to Know You: A Tale of Two People 17
  1. Where Are You Right Now? 20
    Check in with Yourself 21
    What motivates you? 22
  2. What Is Most Important? (Core Values) 25
  3. Your Big 100 List 28
  4. Your Life by Design 35
  5. Your Goals 39
  6. Your Strengths (Identifying Your Superpowers) 43
    Recognizing Your Strengths 47
    Reflection on Strengths 49

Learn to Bounce. Manage Your Energy. Learn to Thrive. 51
  Why Smart People Do Stupid Things (The Stress Reaction) 52
  Self-Check: How Does Stress Affect You? 55
  Your High-Performance Advantage: The Resilience Pyramid 59
    5 Levels of Resilience Assessment 62
    3 Things 74
    Reflection 76
  Resilience: Power Up Your Capacity 77
    Reflection: 78
  Mindfulness as a Daily Practice 79
  Body Scan 82

    The Focus Challenge 83
        One-Minute Shift... 85
        The 20-Minute Rule.. 86
    The Mechanism of Mindset: Awareness. Plan. Action. 86
        100-Day Action Plan.. 89
        Your 100-Day Plan... 90

Emotions, Mindset, and Habits for a No-Excuses Life.....................93
    Fatal Emotions 109
    Drama Triangle 115
    Habits 123
        Infrastructure Habits (The Habits to Build On)........................... 126
        Mindset Habits... 128
    From Autopilot to Power Mindset 129

You, 2.0: A Better, Rewired Version of You 131
    Confidence 133
    Own Your Confidence: Power Pose 136
    Confidence Killers...137
        Your Inner Critic... 138
        Perfectionism... 142
    Stinkin' Thinkin' (Thinking Habits That Sabotage You) 145
    You Are Like the Titanic...149
    Power of Optimism 152

Your Internal GPS: Manage Expectations. Set Boundaries. 154
    Boundaries: Where do you begin and end?.......................................159
        Ways You Can Set Boundaries 164

The Past: The Number-One Barrier to Future Success 168
    Internal Conflict: When Your Future Self Procrastinates.................169

Procrastination *172*

Bias: Mindset Distortion 173

Living Life Deliberately **178**

The Next Step in Visualization...186

Tips for Success.. **189**

Appendix 191

5 Whys..192

Descriptions of the Sixty Strengths...194

Message from Dr. Howard.. **198**

Work Smart Club **200**

About the Author... **202**

Other Books Written by Dr. Howard **203**

Endnotes 204

References **205**

Life Happens: Do You Roll, Bounce, or Get Stuck?

Life goes along, and we learn to adapt to what shows up—until we hit the wall.

This happens to everyone. We've all hit a wall and been stopped in our tracks because of an unexpected experience: losing a job or a spouse, an illness, or an accident. It's usually during these big events that we realize *life happens* (it's not just a cliché). During those experiences, it seems you suddenly become aware of the choices you've made and situations you may have put up with for too long. And life becomes hard.

Now what? Do you roll with the sudden changes and lose the opportunity to have the life you really want? Do you bounce—moving forward into a new way of living life? Or, do you get stuck in the emotional quagmire of "what the bleep just happened?"

How you cope with life events changes how you see yourself. Are you a victim? A martyr? Or, do you choose to learn from this experience and develop your potential?

What's Stopping You Today? is a guide to help you understand yourself as well as a toolbox of proven resources you can use to change how you think, feel, and believe. You will learn to bounce—and become unstoppable.

Why bounce? When you learn to live a deliberate life, you become your own CEO.

Living your life deliberately has less to do with your skills, talents, status, or credentials than it does with your mindset and how you see yourself and the world around you. By choosing to live in a deliberate way, you activate the potential in people, places, and situations and, more importantly, you activate your own potential.

This book and online program will break through the barriers that get in the way of you being your best. While big transitions like divorce and loss have an undeniable impact on our life, the everyday hassles are what gets in the way of you making incremental progress toward your dream and cost you the most.

In the age of information overload, it can get overwhelming trying to find what works. Most people have tried making resolutions or setting goals and failed. This program is different. It offers a formula to understand, learn, and break free. We know it is not about the program. It is all about how you think about yourself.

This program blends science and wisdom with your willingness to look at yourself from a distance. There is more to you than you realize. How much more would be possible if you unlocked that potential?

You will learn the number-one secret—hiding in plain sight—that sabotages most people and keeps them from achieving success. I will share what it is and how to go beyond it. I make this process simple and straightforward. It does, however, require you to be open and willing to journal, reflect, and try something different. I'll help you with that as well.

I want to commend you for wanting to show up at your very best. And rest assured, I know how to get you there. You do not need to keep spinning your wheels trying this and that approach to overcome barriers to living life on your terms.

How You See Yourself Matters More Than Anything You Do

Before you can begin to understand what's stopping you today, you must understand this: your belief system about yourself—who you think you are and what you think you are capable of—is the most powerful force in your life. It can either hold you back or propel you forward.

Everything we do and every experience we have shapes our view of ourselves, especially in today's 24/7 connected world.

We are living longer, staying younger longer, and working longer, which means we will move through more transitions in our lives and careers than any previous generation. These transitions—and how we navigate them—determine how we see ourselves, how relationships and lifestyles flow (or not), and how we take advantage of new opportunities.

24/7 technology has changed how we live, work, and communicate in every facet of our lives. Isn't it interesting that while we're living at a time when we have record levels of information at our fingertips and a social connection with the entire globe, we are less connected and experience more anxiety? We are living with constant distraction, in the age of immediate gratification, fighting off the fear of missing out. Social media presents a perfect world for imperfect people, and there is an expectation to measure up.

The intrusion of technology has compromised certain people skills, increasing misunderstanding and irritability. There is less satisfaction in everyday interactions, and our inner battery is being drained more rapidly than ever with little chance to recharge.

Living in the digital age has also affected the workplace, where there is now more uncertainty than ever. Restructuring of departments and changing roles and responsibilities at work happens regularly, adding to this uncertainty. New technology means learning new skills; we need to update every two years to stay current. You barely get to know your job before you have added responsibilities, leaving many to wonder, what's next? You'll likely have to learn to work with multi-generations and, let's face it, people who are not committed to the job.

Do you have the capacity to perform with incessant demands and the uncertainty of what's next?

Your ability to bounce through the uncertainty, chaos of change, and constant advancements in the digital landscape is one of your most important skill sets. This includes making tough decisions, prioritizing, managing expectations, dealing with grief, forgiving others (mostly yourself), and managing your needs while juggling everyone else's. Being able to focus in the age of distraction requires you to manage your energy during constant change.

But maintaining that focus in and of itself is exhausting. Our inner battery is not being charged. So, we are losing more energy, every day, than we renew.

Think about it: all our devices have an operating system that's updated routinely to deal with the bugs, the interaction of apps and new software. Our nervous system is an operating system, too, but it has not had an upgrade in 100,000 years! We are still motivated by our primitive brain, triggered by the survival instinct of the stress response, causing overreactions in relationships, along with mishaps at work, poor decisions, high blood pressure, weight gain, immune problems, and more.

The needed upgrade for us humans in today's culture is a resilient mindset. When you feel like you have hit the wall, a resilient mindset will give you control and confidence as you experience the transitions of life: the disappointment of a missed opportunity, the sadness of losing someone you love, the pain of a disappointing relationship, or any of the countless other things that zap your energy.

And a resilient mindset begins with what you believe about yourself.

How does your belief system about yourself—and what you are capable of—hold you back?

Regardless of where you are, what age or stage, this program will help you build authentic confidence, transform limiting beliefs, and unlock your potential for greater success, personally and professionally. By following through on this program to discover what's stopping you today, you will dramatically increase your opportunities, as well as your everyday successes.

6 Keys to Energizing Success

"I knew my boss wanted me to work another weekend, but I told my daughter I would take her camping. It seems like he never asks anyone else to work overtime. I don't feel like he takes me seriously."

Doris came to me because she wanted to look for a new job but felt stuck. As a VP of Marketing, she was earning a great salary but was working too much overtime and felt her boss was taking advantage of her.

When I asked her to tell me about herself, she explained, "growing up as a middle child, I felt like I had to always accommodate. I call it the middle child syndrome, going along to get along. My mother was always telling me to not make waves. I guess it stuck."

She needed a new story.

I shared with her the power of branding herself as a leader and changing her story. This program will help you go from doing things the same way you always have, but not accomplishing your goals, to finally getting what you really want in your life.

This book and online program introduce six key areas to unlock your potential and overcome obstacles that keep you from achieving your very best. Finally, a proven approach to get the results you want!

1. **Get to Know You: Learn Why You Can't Move Ahead.**

    It may sound corny, but despite living with yourself, do you really know yourself? Or are you seeing yourself through the lens of labels that others have given you? This is your default story.

Too many times people see themselves through their fears, regrets, and worries. The problem is, this is not the best or authentic you. You were born with innate potential; circumstances may have suppressed it, dulled your shine. I have the keys to move from lack and limitation to possibility.

2. **Learn to Bounce. Manage Your Energy. Learn to Thrive.**

   In the words of Einstein, you cannot think about your future with the same mind that created your past and expect it to be different. You need a resilient mindset. Learn to bounce—forward—from setbacks and challenges. Learn proven strategies to renew your energy and refresh your mindset. Transform your reaction to stress.

3. **Emotions, Mindset and Habits for a No-Excuses Life.**

   Most people go through their days on autopilot. Our brains are hardwired to keep us safe and to be efficient. This makes it challenging to change habits. In this section, you will learn the anatomy of a habit and how to build power habits to transform sabotage into success. You will learn to appreciate your emotions and harness their potential to power up your life.

4. **You, 2.0: A Better, Rewired Version of Yourself.**

   What if you could change your internal programming and instead of running a "fear" scenario, you could upgrade and run the "power of potential" program? Confidence is the way to approach challenges. It is all about how you show up. We'll take you through a process to own it and show up with authentic confidence.

5. **Your Internal GPS: Manage Expectations. Set Boundaries.**

    Most of us rely on the GPS in our phone to find the best route and navigate accidents and traffic problems. This key helps you navigate daily demands and expectations from people who want things quicker, faster and yesterday.

6. **The Past: The Number-One Barrier to Future Success.**

    The past is the number-one barrier to the future. This is true regardless if you've been successful or not. In fact, the more success you've had, the harder it may be to see yourself going beyond that.

This book is supported by an online library of resources: audio, video, templates, checklists, and assessments. Log in. Learn. Grow. Go for it!

This program, *What's Stopping You Today*, will transform self-doubt, confusion, distraction, and pressure into focus with a plan to live life successfully. Transform old habits that do not support your very best and develop new habits that will support the upgraded version of your best self.

How you think about yourself,
how you see yourself,
matters more than anything
else you do.

Get to Know You: A Tale of Two People

Every moment is an opportunity. We have a choice to seize the moment and all it offers or go through the motions and continue along, the way things have always been.

Every moment offers up a brand-new experience—unless you are disconnected from the deeper and divine *you*, the one who recognizes the power of the present moment. One of the most serious consequences of stress and distraction is that you lose your connection to this part of yourself. As technology changes how we live, work, and communicate, distraction is being accepted as the new normal, and the consequences of that can be severe.

Let me introduce you to Leslie. She is a new physician, eager to serve her patients and begin her new life. She found out the hard way the real cost of living life distracted.

While in medical school, she had very clear goals: to complete school and finish at the top of her class. This drove her expectations and fueled her discipline. Once she graduated and began to work, however, she neglected to set up any new goals and instead started work and thought, *Now, it's my turn to live my life.*

Without clear goals, Leslie was saying yes to work responsibilities and life activities without hesitation and quickly herself short on time and energy.

One afternoon, Leslie was in the hospital making rounds and stopped to write new orders for her patient, who had suffered a stroke. She explained, "I was in a hurry because of a meeting I had agreed to that held me up. I let that pressure get to me. I was writing the order for medication and was interrupted by a text. I forgot to double-check my order. The nurse sent the order to the pharmacy as I wrote it. I went on to the next patient."

What Leslie did not know until later was she had forgotten to include blood draws to monitor the medication. The nurse was busy and missed this, as did the pharmacist. All were distracted by the pressure of the busy day.

The patient was on the medication for one month without any monitoring. This was not discovered until he came to his follow-up appointment thirty days later. Fortunately, he did not suffer any negative consequences. When Leslie realized what had happened, she was devastated and began to doubt her ability to be a good physician. She lost trust in herself.

Leslie recognized she needed to have a plan for her life. She was drained and discouraged and doubted her ability to be the physician she always wanted to be. "When I looked at what I had done in medical school, I could see that having a clear vision of what I wanted for my life allowed me to accomplish so much," she said. "I want a new vision for myself; I like being my very best."

To reclaim her focus, Leslie began incorporating simple tools to reboot her attention and was motivated to minimize her distractions. She did not like what had happened to her performance as a result of losing her concentration.

You have a choice when you approach your daily challenges; distraction and confusion obscure this fact. You can interpret your experience through the lens of distraction or with a resilient mindset. Let's compare the two:

Distracted/Limited Mindset	Resilient Mindset
Narrow perspective	Forward focus
Problem focus	Sees possibilities
Isolated	Optimistic
Fear-based, pessimistic	Self-confident
Self-doubt	Purpose driven

It is essential to understand where you are during your day and have the ability to change your course as needed. In this section, you will go through six steps to clarify and identify your values, goals, and strengths so you can energize your success. Moving from a limiting mindset to one of resilience is a choice. You need clarity to make the best choice.

Most people plan their vacations with more detail than they plan their lives. That could be because no one has encouraged life planning, or because it takes too much time, or because it can be a little scary to dig deeper into what you really want.

As an Executive Coach, I have helped many people take the plunge and go through this self-exploration; they came out happier and more focused. This mindset shift can have a lasting impact on the quality of your life. We will walk through this process together so you can define what you want your life to look like.

Let's start right where you are now and move forward to what you want.

1. Where Are You Right Now?

On the chart below give each element a number (0-100) to reflect how close it is to your ideal. On each element, a score of 100 represents the ideal.

Today	**%**	**Ideal**
Job		Job
Family		Family
Love		Love
Money		Money
Creativity		Creativity
Passion		Passion
Opportunity		Opportunity
Health		Health

Check in with Yourself

What activities at work energize you?

_____
_____
_____
_____

What are your strengths?

_____
_____
_____
_____

What activities at work drain your energy?

_____
_____
_____
_____

What do you need to do a great job?

_____
_____
_____

What motivates you?

Rank order this list from the #1 motivator on through #8. You can also grab your card deck and sort the cards.

↑ indicates change increases your motivation   ↓ indicates change decreases your motivation   ~ indicates change has neutral impact

Motivator	Rank Order 1-8	Use arrows/ dash to indicate how change impacts your motivation
Belonging. Being part of the team.		
Progress. Getting work done.		
Purpose. Meaningful work.		
Creativity. Self-expression.		
Quality. Doing it right.		
Appreciation. Recognition for effort.		
Growth. Promotion. Opportunity. $.		
Clarity. Knowing what needs to get done.		

How does change affect your motivation? Look at your motivators on previous page, how are your top 3 impacted with change? Write out your reaction and the consequences of your reaction.

See example:

Example:

#1 Motivator: PROGRESS

When I make progress, I am getting work done.

Impact of Change:
Stalls and slows progress. It is frustrating and my reaction is to push harder, increasing demands on staff and myself.

Putting It Together:

Review your lists and write down the most important contributing factors in each column.

Date/Time	Energized	Drained	Motivators	Strengths

Are there skills you need to move ahead?

1.

2.

3.

4.

2. What Is Most Important? (Core Values)

People tend to be so busy "doing" that they lose touch with what is important. Values bring meaning and purpose to your life and help you make decisions based on what matters most. They represent what is most important to you. Once you have identified these values, making decisions becomes much easier.

On the next two pages, we have provided a list of values. Look at each list and choose three that are essential for you. Then fill in the chart below with the values you have selected. This is not an exhaustive list; write in your own values if not on the main list.

Work | **Personal**

Important

1.   1.

2.   2.

3.   3.

Necessary & Non-Negotiable

1.   1.

2.   2.

3.   3.

Values List: Career/Work

Feel free to write in values that are not on the list.

Achievement	Excellence	Religion
Adventure	Decisiveness	Reputation
Advancement	Power and authority	Leadership
Problem-solving		Meaningful work
Variety	Helping other people	Money
Close relationships	Privacy	Nature
Community	Public service	Wealth
Competence	Honesty	Security (Financial, Otherwise)
Competition	Independence	
Cooperation	Quality	Trust
Country	Influencing others	Self-esteem/self-respect
Efficiency	Inner harmony	
Ethical practice	Recognition	
	Integrity	

Values List: Personal

Feel free to write in values that are not on the list.

Adventure

Affection

Artistic expression

Variety

Close relationships

Community

Cooperation

Country

Connection to earth

Excitement

Fame

Wealth

Stability

Tradition

Sophistication

Friendships

Physical activity

Having a family

Religion

Spiritual connection

Tranquility

Security (Financial or otherwise)

Knowledge/learning

Self-respect

Privacy

Trustworthiness

Winning

Self-awareness

Individuality

Altruism

Now go back and write your values on the list.

3. Your Big 100 List

In this section, let yourself explore all those scenarios that would make you happy, feel fulfilled or provide the life you want. This is YOUR list. Do not hold back.

Think about the following:

- » Places you want to visit
- » Sports you want to try
- » Hobbies you want to pursue
- » Career goals, titles you want to have
- » Things you want to own (Cars. Homes, other toys)
- » Relationships you want to have
- » Financial success (measurable terms)

The following pages have a 100-point list. That may seem overwhelming. It is intended to breakthrough default thinking and expand possibilities. Keep this list handy and continue to add to it. You want to think beyond what you think is possible for you *right now*, and jot down what you may want in the future.

Some of your dreams may be wistful. As you stretch you will discover what truly motivates and inspires you.

If you limit yourself to what is reasonable, or what you think is possible under current circumstances, you forfeit what you really want. You compromise on your dream. Push yourself to get to one hundred.

1.
2.
3.
4.
5.
6.
7.
8.
9.
10.
11.
12.
13.
14.
15.
16.
17.
18.
19.
20.

21. ___
22. ___
23. ___
24. ___
25. ___
26. ___
27. ___
28. ___
29. ___
30. ___
31. ___
32. ___
33. ___
34. ___
35. ___
36. ___
37. ___
38. ___
39. ___
40. ___

41.
42.
43.
44.
45.
46.
47.
48.
49.
50.
51.
52.
53.
54.
55.
56.
57.
58.
59.
60.

61.
62.
63.
64.
65.
66.
67.
68.
69.
70.
71.
72.
73.
74.
75.
76.
77.
78.
79.
80.

81.
82.
83.
84.
85.
86.
87.
88.
89.
90.
91.
92.
93.
94.
95.
96.
97.
98.
99.
100.

Do you have 100?

Some of these dreams are wistful, and some may not be a focus for you right now. The point of doing this is to stretch your thinking, break through your default status quo. Open to possibilities.

Dream BIG.

4. Your Life by Design

In this section, you will lay out what you want your life to look like. Answer the following questions:

What do you want to accomplish this year?

_____

_____

How much money do you want to make?

_____

What lifestyle do you want?

_____

_____

_____

Where do you want to live?

_____

_____

_____

What skills/education do you need to accomplish your goals?

_____

_____

_____

Once you have answered the questions, you can set up your short list of goals/dreams. Based on the previous questions, what is most important to you now? *It may only be one main goal.*

1.

2.

3.

4.

5.

6.

7.

Now you have a good idea of what you want to focus on for the next year. You can go through your list and put a date on them or categorize them based on the initial life elements in the Alignment exercise.

Next, let's look at ways you may be sabotaging your dreams based on daily choices you are making.

Do your DAILY CHOICES match your desired outcome?

Go through your day and look at the choices you make and how aligned they are with your desired outcomes.

What changes do you need to make in your daily choices?

I will do less of:

1.

2.

3.

I will do more of:

1.

2.

3.

Think about your job choices and other decisions you are making. Are they aligned with what you really want? What do you need to do to center your decision on your values and dreams? Write it out.

5. Your Goals

Did you know ninety percent of people do not achieve their goals? They get distracted, or the goals seem too hard or impossible, so the goals end up delayed, diluted, or discarded all together.

Do you relate?

Let's look at some of the reasons people fail to achieve their goals.

The goals are too vague.

Goals that are not measurable are not sticky. If you do not know when you'll arrive, you'll have less motivation to work for it. By human nature, you'll only try when you're sure you can achieve what you have set out to achieve.

Solution: Make your goals specific and measurable. What will you see that lets you know you have arrived at your goal?

The goals lack relevance and meaning.

Meaning and purpose are the top drivers of motivation. Knowing your "why" will keep you focused on the end result, even when you may have lost that lovin' feeling for your goal. After the honeymoon period wears off and you are faced with challenges related to achieving your goal, you need to have a strong "why" to keep from quitting.

Solution: Use the 5 Whys to get to the fundamental reason you are doing what you are doing. Not sure about the 5 Whys? Check the Appendix.

The nays have it.

Goals and plans can bring out the naysayers. *Your goals are yours.* They do not require consensus or approval. Even well-intentioned friends and family can discourage you from going for it. Other people might be jealous or negative and seek to hold you back so you won't make them look bad.

Too many worthy goals are lost because friends, family, and naysayers end up influencing your thoughts.

Solution: Find your why (done in the previous step) and keep that in the front of your mind. Work on self-approval and wean yourself from needing the approval of others. This makes the naysayers less persuasive.

Procrastination.

This shows up in different ways. Perfectionists struggle with putting things off because if it cannot be done perfectly, then they continue to "work on it" until they feel ready. Unfortunately, that time never comes.

Solution: The above suggestions will help with procrastination. If you do struggle with perfectionism, acknowledge and work on that. We cover this in the online work and well-being center, the Work Smart Club.

Too much to do (including distractions).

When you have too much to do, it could be due to your inability to say no, as well as a lack of clarity about what you should actually be doing. It is easy to take on jobs and responsibilities when you lack the clarity around what is most important.

Solution: Clarifying the values that drive you will help you say no to the activities that don't support your core. Spend time deciding what you need to be busy doing.

Researchers have found that plans that contain incremental goals are more motivating. People achieve these goals more quickly than with a broadly stated long-term plan. This partly due to the ability to connect the dots between the plan and the outcome. Making progress is one of the top motivators, so having smaller goals can be a key driver of performance.

Also, shorter goals are more flexible and can be revised as needed. This flexibility is encouraging. Life happens, and most do not want to be locked into a plan that stops working. In fact, researchers have found that when plans conflict, rumination replaces creativity.

Suggestion: Set up 30-day plans with 10-day incremental steps. Watch what happens to your performance.

Breaking down your goals into milestones and smaller steps will require more time, but it is well worth it. This extra time ensures you will achieve your desired outcome and avoid the stops and starts that happen with unclear goals.

According to research on the world's most common strength and weakness:

The most common strength is the desire to make a difference.

The most common weakness is the inability to overcome fears and do what is necessary. [8]

People want to make a difference in the world and experience meaning in their lives, yet a third of people—worldwide—struggle to overcome their fear of doing it.

Read on ... let's break through.

6. Your Strengths (Identifying Your Superpowers)

Do you think about the things you're good at? Or do you concentrate on your weaknesses, thinking by focusing on your weaknesses you will improve your overall performance?

After going through this section, you will understand how focusing on your strengths can power up your success in amazing ways. Most people are taught to focus on their weaknesses to be "well-rounded." This leaves you drained and de-motivated, with little to add to your strengths. This may be why you feel stuck.

Research into strengths (as opposed to focusing on weaknesses) found that people who focus on their strengths are:

- happier
- more confident
- more energetic
- less stressed
- more resilient
- more likely to achieve their goals
- better performing at work and are more engaged
- learning more quickly

That is powerful! And to get there you need a mindset shift.

I will show you how you can have more energy, influence, and enjoyment by focusing on your strengths. You will transform your mindset from being stuck on limitations to one that sees possibility.

Ready? Let's look at how to quickly transform your mindset.

When you took the Strengths Profile, you received a report that outlined sixty different characteristics in four categories: *Realized Strengths*, *Unrealized Strengths*, *Learned Behaviors*, and *Weaknesses*. I like this assessment because it recognizes *energy* as a defining force; your strengths are what you do well and what energize you. I will explain more about what the categories mean so you get the most from your report.

> **Energy is what makes your life, relationships, dreams flourish. It is the fuel behind passion.**

Passion is what drives you to pursue your dreams through the challenges and roadblocks that show up every day. Engage your strengths, and you will energize your success. Focus on weaknesses or areas that do not energize you, and you will quickly lose your mojo, flattening your view of what you can do. This is dangerous.

Workplace research has shown that most people do not feel they utilize their strengths on the job. This can happen because many people do not really know their strengths when they set out looking for a job, and others ignore them in order to stay in the job, usually out of fear of doing something different.

Too often, you end up over-using your learned behaviors—things you do well but do not energize you—at work, and you burn out. This also happens in business, relationships, and life. Remember, your energy is what allows your success to flourish; without it, it is easier to doubt yourself, underperform, and lose interest.

Remember Doris, VP of Marketing? She wanted to look for a new job, but she felt stuck. She explained it this way: "I am making a great salary I'm not sure I can replace. I am good at managing details, but it drains me. I keep track of the department's numbers and make sure we meet our goals. What I really love the most about my job is coaching my staff. But I do not get to do that very much."

I suggested Doris take the Strengths Profile to help her see what energizes her and how she might redefine her current role or open up possibilities for her career. Doris said she "loved" coaching her staff, giving me a clue that she would benefit from a position that enabled more relationship building. Her Strengths Profile revealed the following:

Strengths	Learned Behavior	Weaknesses
Rapport Builder	Detail	Competitive
Listener		Incubator
Growth		

Doris was relieved when she saw her profile. "This makes sense," she said. "I was doubting my ability to do my job because I had lost interest in reviewing reports. Now, I understand that while I am good at detail, it does not energize me. When I combined my need to engage *Detail*, one of my learned behaviors, with the intense review of the data, I was literally drained. The strength *Incubator* was one of my weaknesses."

Descriptions of the sixty strengths are listed in the Appendix. If you have taken the assessment, grab your report and check out the explanations there as well.

Doris and I worked together to "redesign" her role and responsibilities. When you find out your strengths, it is important to honor the information so you can show up at your very best.

Successful people operate from their strengths the majority of the time.

As you learn what your strengths are, look for ways you can redesign your current role. You may be able to find someone who complements your weaknesses, and can share the responsibilities that drain you, while you take on those that drain your partner. Or, you can always look for a new position that more closely matches your strengths.

Doris liked the people she worked with, and wanted to stay in her current role, if possible. She was able to find the right person with "*Detail*" as a strength to prepare the reports, and she worked with him to provide her expertise in the review process. She coached and mentored this person for a future leadership role.

This energized both of them and supported her company as well. Win-win-win.

Knowing the power of strength building, she developed a coaching plan for her team. As she became more energized in the process, her boss took notice. Doris explained, "I used to think my boss did not take me seriously, but he noticed the increased engagement in my team and complimented me. At some point, I will explain more about the power of operating from your strengths to him. Who knows? Maybe I can create a new project!"

Focusing on your strengths will help you rewrite your story.

It did for Doris. She had more energy and was more positive and much stronger as a leader. She recognized the strengths in others and was able to help her team redesign their roles to complement them. This increased their satisfaction on the job—and their respect for Doris. More work got done without people being exhausted.

Identifying your innate strengths will allow you to flourish. Operating from your strengths literally magnetizes your performance and increases your satisfaction—even when things get tough.

Recognizing Your Strengths

Learning to operate from your strengths does take a mindset shift. Most people confuse what they are good at with their strengths. This only tells part of the story, if what you are good at also energizes you, then you have identified a strength. Begin to think in terms of what energizes you and what does not.

Use the following chart to help you spot strengths in yourself and others.[7]

Note	Note
What did you like to do as a child that you still enjoy doing?	What energizes you when you are engaged in that activity?
Are there things you have picked up quickly?	What makes you feel like the "real" you when engaged in it?
Where does your attention naturally go?	What motivates you? What do you do because you love to do it?

Because many people (and organizations) focus on their weaknesses, people do not learn to distinguish between skills, talents and true strengths. In fact, many spend most of their working life doing something they are good at but that doesn't energize them.

The assessment, Strength Profile refers to the Learned behaviors (LB) as things you do well, but they do not energize you. They may have been strengths at one point, but they were overused. You still perform them well, but they do not energize you. It could be the current situation you are in has made this particular strength no longer motivating.

Remember Doris? She was paid well because of her learned behavior, *Detail*. However, it was overused, and when combined with other aspects of her job that relied on her weaknesses, she became depleted. By shifting her focus to her strengths and finding a way to compensate for learned behaviors and weaknesses, she began to overperform. She learned a new way to see her value and the value in her team. This happened with just a slight shift in how she thought about getting work done.

Let's explore *Weaknesses*. These are activities that you do not perform well *and* they drain your energy. Weaknesses are often the focus for personal and professional development. Think about it: if weaknesses drain your energy, how long can you endure the training before you lose interest and give up? And how might this strain your work in general?

> **You cannot have expectations for an amazing life if you are mired in weaknesses and lacking the energy to move ahead.**

The best way to deal with weaknesses is to acknowledge them. You have to recognize areas that can derail your success or limit your progress. Without awareness of your strengths, weaknesses, and learned behaviors, you'll draw unfair conclusions about your own abilities.

When considering your weaknesses, think about the overall impact a weakness has on your performance. Is it a mission critical aspect of what you need to do? Can your strengths help balance this? Can you redesign your role? Is there someone you can partner with to balance out this weakness?

Because you are learning to recognize your value and how you might approach your job, or your business, from a different perspective, you open up the possibility of tapping into your hidden potential. This is what the Strengths Profile calls your *Unrealized Strengths.*

Tap into these strengths that are not being used and expand your possibilities.

Reflection on Strengths

How might your day change if you had more energy?

_____

_____

_____

What would you love to do if you had the energy to do it? List one thing:

_____

Rewrite your story. Control your future.

Go to the online course, and work through this module. It will help you identify your superpower!

Change your reaction to stress,
and you will change your entire life.

Learn to Bounce. Manage Your Energy. Learn to Thrive.

To get more done, most people think about longer hours, giving it greater effort and pushing through whatever challenge shows up. When you learn to manage your attention (and your energy) you will focus on your goals and get more done without exhausting yourself.

Having to get more done with less is normal but burning the dandle at both ends only burns out you and the candle. This is what happened to Laetitia. Listen to what happened, in her words:

"I just started my new role. I was promoted to Director of a new department. I created this department with my boss. We were the only ones in the county doing this and I wanted to keep the momentum going. In my excitement, I lost track of the rest of my life; my partner, my kids and me. I kept saying, *I am almost done.* Yet, there was always one more thing."

> **Newsflash: There will always be 24 hours in a day. Cutting back on sleep, family time and other healthy habits to "get more done" is not a long-term solution.**

There is nothing wrong with working hard to more your agenda forward. What is wrong is to think that your effort and energy alone will be all you need. Before long, pushing harder becomes a habit and you lose perspective and stop searching for an innovative way to move ahead. Isolation, resentment and exhaustion sets in.

How well you focus will determine what you achieve and how much you enjoy it We all feel better, satisfied and more competent when we see results. Stop and ask yourself, does pushing harder get me the results I really want?

Do you relate?

Why Smart People Do Stupid Things (The Stress Reaction)

Stress changes perception. The stress reaction is part of the body's survival instinct. We are hardwired to react to threats.

Just the other day, one of my clients found herself scared and overreacting when she encountered a dog on her afternoon walk. It was a small dog on a leash. Years ago, she was attacked by a large, menacing dog and it was this memory that triggered this current overreaction. When she came back from the walk, she snapped at her assistant, who happened to ask, "*How was your walk?*" Deep in thought, distracted, my client had been caught off-guard and was not even aware of her aggressive response. She also wasn't aware that her assistant shut down when she snapped it her.

Our nervous system is designed for survival and is hardwired to respond with the flight/fight response to ensure survival. The threat can be real or imagined—the reaction is the same. Unchecked and chronic stress creates a hypervigilance and your nervous system reacts to everything as a threat.

> **Unchecked stress is a major energy leak that uses up your precious resources. As distraction increases, the stress reaction also increases.**

If you have been caught by surprise and found yourself over-reacting to something, it is because the primitive part of your brain was triggered. The stress reaction is a primitive survival response; first you feel, then you think.

The "Fast-Track" of the stress response is when the stressor triggers the survival instinct and your logical, analytic, rational part of the brain is unavailable. Your thinking cortex's ability to decide about the stressor is overridden by the primitive, fast-track process of this survival instinct. We all have filters from the past through which all new experiences are perceived.

The primitive brain includes the amygdala, responsible for decoding threats and perceiving the emotions of fear, anger and sadness. It stores memories of events and emotions to protect you from future *perceived* threats. If you *imagine* that something is a threat, your nervous system goes onto the flight or fight reaction.

Did your boss say something that left you wondering about your performance? Angry at what that customer said? You are likely triggered and ready to explode—unless you tune into what you are experiencing and act.

Add distraction into the interaction and you have greater potential to be hijacked; you end up having to do damage control at work.

The link from the part of your brain acting like a security guard (amygdala) to the thinking brain (cortex) is much stronger and well-developed than the link *from* your thinking brain to the amygdala. **This means that your stress reaction is going to be stronger and faster than your thought to stop it.** Most of the reactions people have at work, as well as in personal relationships, are a result of this trigger.

Think about a recent time you overreacted. What was going on prior to that? Think back 24 hours. Write it out.

_____
_____
_____
_____
_____
_____
_____

Self-Check: How Does Stress Affect You?

The following represents ways that stress can show up. Check all that apply. Knowing what your body talk is communicating to you will help you also know what to do next.

Physical Reaction to Stress

Symptom	Frequency & Severity: Daily Weekly Monthly 1-10 (10= Severe)	Symptom	Frequency & Severity: Daily Weekly Monthly 1-10 (10= Severe)
Headaches		Sweating	
Joint Pain		Rapid Heart Rate	
Heartburn		Colds, Flu	
Indigestion		Sinus Trouble	
Fatigue		Irregular Heart Rate	
Constipation		Forgetfulness	
Neck Pain		Concentration Difficulty	

If you checked three or more boxes, there are lifestyle changes needed to avoid more serious health challenges. Chronic, unchecked stress contributes to premature aging. We want you to set up a self-care program to address these and other signs of chronic stress.

Emotional/Spiritual Signs of Stress

Symptoms	Frequency & Severity: Daily Weekly Monthly 1-10 (10= Severe)	Symptoms	Frequency & Severity Daily Weekly Monthly 1-10 (10= Severe)
Tension		Worry	
Irritability		Loss of Motivation	
Depression		Cynical/Sarcastic	
Anger		Weight Gain	
Rage		Food Cravings	
Call Out Sick		Can't Fall Asleep	
Can't Stay Asleep		Racing Thoughts	
Negative		Pessimistic	
Want to Run Away		Isolates from Friends	
Never Enough Time		Could Jump Out of My Skin	
Addicted to Facebook		Increased Alcohol Use	
Wake Up Tired Even After 8 Hours Sleep		Work Shifts and Rotates Days and Night Shift	

What stands out to you as you look at the chart you just completed?

What can you **today** to decrease your stressful feelings?

THE 5 LEVELS OF RESILIENCE

Your High-Performance Advantage: The Resilience Pyramid

During my coaching practice I recognized a pattern in those individuals who successfully moved beyond burnout and the pressure-performance roller coaster typical in high stakes careers. The Resilience Pyramid is the map I developed after working with thousands of clients who successfully reclaimed their personal power.

I call it your high-performance advantage because when you learn to manage your energy, increase your awareness, you open to impactful skills of resilient mindset, influence and flow.

Here are the five levels to build resilience:

5. **Master Your Energy**

    This is the foundation of the pyramid; your physical vitality and stamina. In this level you look at your lifestyle habits and choices; do they support the energy levels you need for what is demanded of you?

    Are you ramping up your energy with coffee during the day only to be wound up at night and then not sleep well? Are you using wine, food or other measures to manage your emotions?

    Start with the basics: drink more water, increase vegetables and fruits with plenty of fiber, get 15 minutes of exercise every day, get the right amount of sleep for you and engage in prayer or meditation to center your mind.

4. Stress Tolerance

This is the level most people talk about when they talk about resilience. What you do in step one will improve your stress tolerance. This is not your ability to tough it out. White knuckling your way through a tough spot has its limits and eventually the pressure erodes your ability to handle it.

Building stress tolerance is about *having awareness* of how stress impacts you and then putting a plan in place to help you avoid the negative consequences of the stress reaction.

Your ability to manage your stress influences your ability to make decisions, problem solve and communicate effectively. It is an important dimension in emotional intelligence. This level requires awareness to build new habits and ways of responding when under pressure.

3. Mindset: Resilient Thinking

This is an outgrowth of healthy constructive behaviors that you adopt in Levels 4 and 5. It is a specific way of thinking that allows you to be forward, future focused versus in the past, worrying about what happened.

Once you learn to strategically use your mind (versus react because of the stress reaction), you will have access to more of your internal resources to move through challenges *and* take advantage of opportunities. Without this, most people overwork the left sides of their brains, known for its ability to handle limited amounts of data, so they physically push themselves through the challenge, only to crash and burn later.

The fact is, the way you see yourself dramatically affects how you view the world. It is not what is happening to you that determines the outcome, it is how you view it.[1]

Chronic stress creates a perspective that problems are bigger than you are. Think about what happens to your perspective when you are fighting to keep your head above water?

The truth is, most people feel the best when they are "productive," and today's busyness does not provide the satisfaction of accomplishment.

Resilient thinking is a discipline that stops the energy drain of overthinking, bravado, denial, worry, fear, and distraction. Learning to deliberately engage your mind to think more deeply, carefully and systematically will put you in the resilient mindset. This is your secret weapon for better performance and work-life satisfaction.

2. Influence: Your Capacity to Lead and Empower Others

As you activate your resilience on a regular basis, you are managing your emotions and have increased awareness. This frees up your internal resources to be there for someone else.

Most people I have coached want to make a difference in their world. At this level of the pyramid YOU are the difference.

You have learned to manage your energy, set boundaries, identify and manage emotions, and this has increased your capacity to contribute to meaningful projects, support others and influence your world.

This influence goes beyond your leadership position and is experienced by others through your involvement. Be the difference maker. Inspire. Contribute. Influence others to be their best.

1. **Flow**

   Flow is a state of being where you are totally involved in the activity. Have you ever been lost in the moment, losing touch with time? Flow happens naturally, however with increased distraction and the pressure of too much to do, it can be difficult to access.

   As you master each step of the pyramid, you will enter into flow more easily. Flow is regenerative; it is a natural antidote to burnout and engages the whole person. As you spend less time in over reaction, overwhelm and the stress reaction, you will have more energy and the ability to enjoy what you are doing.

5 Levels of Resilience Assessment

This self-assessment helps you tune in to the five levels of the resilience pyramid. I created this pyramid after working with thousands of individuals and noticing a pattern in how people activated their resilience.

Evaluate yourself and answer based on the one (low) to ten (high) scale. Think about your life overall and average your responses.

To score each section, add up the numbers given to each question and divide by ten.

Energy

1. I exercise at least twenty minutes four out of seven days.   1 2 3 4 5 6 7 8 9 10

2. I eat vegetables and fruit daily; minimum of three servings.   1 2 3 4 5 6 7 8 9 10

3. I drink at least eight eight-ounce glasses of water each day.   1 2 3 4 5 6 7 8 9 10

4. For every fast food meal eaten in a week, subtract a point from the total of ten (i.e., 1x, 2x, 3x a day X days of the week).   1 2 3 4 5 6 7 8 9 10

5. I wake up feeling rested.   1 2 3 4 5 6 7 8 9 10

6. I drink coffee or energy drinks to get going. Subtract a point for every drink to boost energy in the week.   1 2 3 4 5 6 7 8 9 10

7. I am satisfied with my weight.   1 2 3 4 5 6 7 8 9 10

8. I have maintained my weight in the last month.   1 2 3 4 5 6 7 8 9 10

9. I have all the energy I need to do what I have to do in the day.   1 2 3 4 5 6 7 8 9 10

10. I have the energy to be creative.   1 2 3 4 5 6 7 8 9 10

TOTAL _____ ÷ 10 = _____

What can you change or add that will have the most impact on your energy?

Stress Tolerance (Self Care)

1. I take care of myself first and then take care of others.   1 2 3 4 5 6 7 8 9 10
2. I receive as much as I give in my personal relationships.   1 2 3 4 5 6 7 8 9 10
3. I make time for my needs.   1 2 3 4 5 6 7 8 9 10
4. I can say no without feeling guilty.   1 2 3 4 5 6 7 8 9 10
5. I spend money on personal development.   1 2 3 4 5 6 7 8 9 10
6. I think about what I need throughout the day.   1 2 3 4 5 6 7 8 9 10
7. I build in time for hobbies every week.   1 2 3 4 5 6 7 8 9 10
8. I am aware of when I need "me" time.   1 2 3 4 5 6 7 8 9 10
9. I easily communicate my needs to others and respect their needs.   1 2 3 4 5 6 7 8 9 10
10. I look at myself in the mirror and enjoy what I see.   1 2 3 4 5 6 7 8 9 10

TOTAL ____ ÷ 10 = ____

What can you do every day to grow?

Mindset

1. I have all the time I need in a day.		1 2 3 4 5 6 7 8 9 10
2. I see the glass half-full.		1 2 3 4 5 6 7 8 9 10
3. I am in charge of my personal life.		1 2 3 4 5 6 7 8 9 10
4. I am in charge of my professional life.		1 2 3 4 5 6 7 8 9 10
5. I easily adapt to the daily challenges that show up.		1 2 3 4 5 6 7 8 9 10
6. I manage stress well.		1 2 3 4 5 6 7 8 9 10
7. I balance the demands in my day and give myself time.		1 2 3 4 5 6 7 8 9 10
8. I bounce back from setbacks.		1 2 3 4 5 6 7 8 9 10
9. I acknowledge mistakes and/or failures and keep going.		1 2 3 4 5 6 7 8 9 10
10. I show up every day and do the best I can.		1 2 3 4 5 6 7 8 9 10

TOTAL ____ ÷ 10 = ____

Do you need to adjust your attitude? In what way?

Influence

1. I make time to spend with my family.   1 2 3 4 5 6 7 8 9 10

2. I am happy with the amount of time spent with friends.   1 2 3 4 5 6 7 8 9 10

3. I make time for my partner every day.   1 2 3 4 5 6 7 8 9 10

4. I make time to talk with my children about what is happening in their lives.   1 2 3 4 5 6 7 8 9 10

5. I make the time to get to know my coworkers and/or my staff.   1 2 3 4 5 6 7 8 9 10

6. I like myself and I am comfortable with who I am.   1 2 3 4 5 6 7 8 9 10

7. I am satisfied with my closest relationships.   1 2 3 4 5 6 7 8 9 10

8. I have fun in my personal relationships.   1 2 3 4 5 6 7 8 9 10

9. I am productive in my work relationships.   1 2 3 4 5 6 7 8 9 10

10. My relationships are balanced in give and take.   1 2 3 4 5 6 7 8 9 10

TOTAL ____ ÷ 10 = ____

How can you improve your relationships?

Flow

1. I engage in a daily spiritual practice with prayer, meditation, and mindfulness.   1 2 3 4 5 6 7 8 9 10

2. I am guided by core values in my daily life.   1 2 3 4 5 6 7 8 9 10

3. I make choices based on my values.   1 2 3 4 5 6 7 8 9 10

4. I feel fulfilled.   1 2 3 4 5 6 7 8 9 10

5. I volunteer my time.   1 2 3 4 5 6 7 8 9 10

6. I support causes important to me with time or money.   1 2 3 4 5 6 7 8 9 10

7. I "unplug" every four hours for at least fifteen minutes.   1 2 3 4 5 6 7 8 9 10

8. I enjoy quiet time in nature.   1 2 3 4 5 6 7 8 9 10

9. I spend time alone and reflect on my life and accomplishments.   1 2 3 4 5 6 7 8 9 10

10. I am inspired by the miracles that show up in my life.   1 2 3 4 5 6 7 8 9 10

TOGETHER _____ ÷ 10 = _____

TOTAL _____ ÷ 10 = _____

What can you do to bring more meaning into your life?

How to Plot Your Scores

Use this graph to plot your scores from each section. Take a highlighter and highlight the number associated with your score, in each of the five categories (round up if needed.) This gives you a quick visual to see what sections have low scores and may require more attention from you.

Make a note in each column about what is working at this level of resilience, or not working.

10					
9					
8					
7					
6					
5					
4					
3					
2					
1					
SCORE	Energy	Self-Care	Mindset	Influence	Flow

Sample Chart with Scores

	Energy	Self-Care Awareness	Mindset	Influence	Flow
10					
9					
8		*Tuned in and aware of how stress impacts my body.*			*I want to be more focused on my goals than absorbed in my problems.*
7	*Increased fast food. Not enough water.*			*When I manage my interruptions, I am more available to my team.*	
6					
5					
4			*Conflict increases my negativity.*		
3					
2					
1					

What Your Scores Mean

I have broken this into sections based on the level of the pyramid.

Energy Management

This level of the resilience pyramid is about your daily choices and how you manage your energy through, food, exercise, sleep, water; the basics of a healthy lifestyle.

If you scored:

<5: You are at risk for increased reaction to stressful events. Without the fuel your body needs to maintain your stamina, there is a tendency to use coffee, sugars, tobacco and other stimulants to keep going. This sets up a vicious cycle. You could be in a cycle of crash and burn or perpetual slow motion, not accomplishing what you would like to get done.

6-8: You are focused, *most of the time*, and able to make choices that support your energy needs. Look at your answers, where is the energy leak? Does it show up with diet, what you drink, your movement or lack of, or your sleep?

>8.5: Congratulations, you can maintain certain disciplines that work for you regarding daily lifestyle choices. It is important to have a plan to keep them up.

Stress Tolerance

The second level of the resilience pyramid has to do with your ability to manage your stress. This level is really about self-awareness. If you do not know how situations (and people) impact you, how can you change how you respond?

If you scored:

<5: You are not tuned into your preferences and your needs. This increases the risk of being hijacked by the stress reaction and being drained. This course will help you learn more about you and provide proven self-care practices you can use in just minutes a day.

6-8 You are learning more about your needs and making a conscious effort to take care of you. On what questions did you score the lowest? I hope you will share on the Coaching Calls, or in the Facebook group; we can offer you suggestions.

>8.5: Congratulations, you are managing your stress and aware of what you need. Be sure to set up a plan to keep it up.

Mindset

The third level of the resilience pyramid has to do with how you think. Do you maintain your perspective when under pressure? What you think, believe and feel drives your actions and your presence as a leader.

If you scored:

<5: You may be struggling with maintaining your perspective. Did you know you can learn to be optimistic?

6-8: You have success with forward perspective, *sometimes*, but may be caught by unchecked pressure. Read through the questions and jot down the circumstances in which you scored low. In this course, you will learn proven tools that will transform your stress reaction and increase your resilience. This is the first step to a resilient mindset and consistently maintaining it.

>8.5: Congratulations, you are staying resilient and your perspective is focused on possibility. Now set up a daily plan to keep your mindset resilient.

Influence

The fourth level of the resilience pyramid is focused on relationships. This is your ability to influence and your awareness of the importance of connections. Every level will build on the next one. As you consistently take care of you, being able to focus on others is natural and easier.

If you scored:

<5: Have you shut down and withdrawn due to increased pressure? You may be under reacting or withholding your emotions or have stopped sharing your feelings because of the increased pressure. This course offers you proven steps to unhook from the debilitating pressure of unchecked stress.

6-8: You have learned to balance results with relationships however still tend to sacrifice the opportunity to connect authentically with people at work or intimately with those closest to you. Stay tuned. In this course you will learn to increase your awareness and mindfulness, making your ability to authentically connect with others easier.

>8.5: Yay! You are staying connected with others at work and in your personal life. Now set up your plan to ensure you do not lose those connections.

Flow

The final level of the resilience pyramid is where you have mastered daily choices, managed your mindset, connected with others and now can go through your day in flow. This is the state of mind where you are focused on what is important and connected to the purpose behind the mission.

Flow is a state of mind that occurs naturally. Most people have had the experience of losing the sense of time when involved in an activity. As you learn to build your resilience you will be able to deliberately engage flow for greater satisfaction at work and in your close relationships.

If you scored:

<5: Are you super focused on getting it all done? Have you lost your curiosity or wonder at every day miracles? Do you avoid spending time alone? Compulsive busyness is not a long-term strategy to get more done.

6-8: You are actively mindful and tuned into your values, making time to review and reflect. There still may be a tendency to solve other people's problems, losing touch with your own purpose and mission.

>8.5: You have learned to FOCUS while still maintaining relationships. You are enjoying challenges. What do you need to do more of, and less of, to consistently engage flow?

The Resilience Roadmap is a way to think about the full scope of resilience. It is not a destination, rather you will travel back and forth between the levels. Stay open and continue to learn more about what works for you and what does not. This system requires a few minutes of daily practice for a profound shift in mindset. This course will move you ahead and give you easy to use, proven tools, backed by science, so you can get more done without burning up or out.

3 Things

Having gone through the assessment, were you able to identify daily choices or behaviors that drain your energy? Or keep you from achieving your goals—consistently?

You have identified things you are doing now, that work well for you. As you eliminate the destructive choices and behaviors, what can you DO MORE of to *consistently* achieve your goals?

Do you manage your energy and time well? What habits are you guilty of and what will you agree to change?

Complete this chart. Think carefully about what you do. This is your program, be honest with you!

3 Things I Will Do More of to energize me	3 Things I Will Do Less of that drain my energy
1.	1.
2.	2.
3.	3.

The Resilience Roadmap in Practice...

This is a very quick and simple example of how you can engage the five levels in your day.

1. Imagine yourself starting the day by tuning into yourself and setting your intention (Influence): *Just for today, I will not anger...*
2. Drink a glass of water with fresh lemon vs coffee. Breathe more slowly and deeply than usual, for three minutes (Energize).
3. Smile more at people you see on the street or in your office. (Flow).
4. Spend your lunch in a mindfulness state of mind as you eat (Self-care).
5. Regardless of the events, keep a positive attitude (Mindset).

On the next pags are Journal prompts. How will you put the roadmap into practice? Keep it simple!

Reflection

Reflect and write about what you learned taking the Resilience Assessment. What do you see or understand about your daily choices and behaviors as you go through your day?

_____
_____
_____
_____
_____
_____
_____
_____

How will you put the Resilience Roadmap into practice?

Energy management · Self Care (Awareness) · Mindset · Relationships (Influence) · Flow

_____
_____
_____
_____
_____
_____
_____

Resilience: Power Up Your Capacity

Resilience is a set of skills you develop in order to show up at your best during challenging times. Resilience is like any muscle; the more you practice tools and techniques that build resilience, the stronger your ability to shift out of the stress reaction and the easier to activate resilience.

On the membership site you have access to audio/ video that will takes you through strategies that will change your reaction to stress, in the moment. Regular use of these tools has amazing benefit including:

- better focus
- improved sleep
- increased intuition
- improved decision making

Resilience is more than "bouncing back." It is the ability to bounce forward into something new.

Think of resilience as your capacity.

Capacity is how much of something you have. Just like your smart phone, when you have a fully charged battery, you can use all the apps and maximize the use of your phone.

Take a moment and reflect on the following questions.

Reflection:

What is it like for you when you are resilient? What do you notice?

What could you accomplish with greater capacity? Identify one thing you want to achieve but fall short due to lack of energy.

Mindfulness as a Daily Practice

One of the complaints I hear frequently is the inability to stop racing thoughts. Lynn, a mother and business owner shared this story: "I start my day running. First thing, I get the kids ready and get texts when my office opens. This doesn't leave any time to breathe! I end up revving myself up on coffee all morning. By the end of the day, I can't turn my mind off."

Throughout the book, I have been talking about the false sense of urgency that happens with chronic distraction. In Lynn's mind, she could not spare fifteen minutes for herself to center her mind and plan her day. I introduced her to mindfulness, as a practice to use during her day.

Being present in the moment is called *mindfulness*. Before technology intruded into life, this was normal. Today, more than ever, people are struggling. The more distracted you are, the more distracted you get, and the more stressed you feel. When emotions are free floating, you become more irritable, there is a tendency to be overwhelmed, and clear thinking disintegrates.

Lynn agreed: "I could not understand why I was so tense with my daughter. She is always asking questions and wants to talk. I was snapping at her. And then I would feel so bad about myself." It is easy to miss the level of distraction and its impact on people around you until, you stop for moment and take notice.

Mindfulness is simply the practice of bringing your wandering mind into the present moment and holding it there. It takes practice. Some people use their breath to bring them into the present. Others focus their attention on an activity in the moment like walking, sitting, breathing, or washing dishes. It can be whatever you are doing, in this moment.

The present moment is three seconds. This is enough time to take a deep breath and experience whatever is happening. Three seconds. A friend of mine is a chef and he explained this is what he does to savor the dish: how does it look, what does it smell like, how do the flavors blend, what is the texture like in that first bite?

The practice of mindfulness recognizes you control your mind and your thoughts. You can be deliberate and slow down your internal processes to get more out of what is happening in the moment. Savor!

It is natural for your mind to introduce thoughts, questions, and even urgent nudges to disrupt your ability to be present. Without a practice of keeping yourself in the moment, it is easy to feel scattered and somewhat agitated, or the opposite—flat. The more you practice mindfulness, you will notice that you become more neutral and observant. This is your goal. You will get more done, take in more information and experience greater satisfaction.

What would it be like if you could go through your day without reacting to other people's needs or feeling rushed without enough time to get anything done?

As you engage in your activities throughout the day, keep your mind in the present moment. When you notice yourself thinking ahead or about something else, get back to the present. We have suggestions on how to do this.

It takes practice to learn to savor and be fully present.

Power Tips for Mindfulness Practice

1. Be patient with yourself. Staying present takes practice. Start with fifteen seconds of bringing your attention into the present and gradually increase your time. With consistent practice, this gets easier and you build resilience.
2. Set your timer for five different times during your day to alert you this is time for an Attention Reboot, deep breathing, visualization, etc. Putting these activities into your calendar increases their importance.
3. Practice the Attention Reboot. Let's say you are in a staff meeting. You don't like being there because it takes time away from finishing up your work. In the past, to avoid feeing the resentment, your mind wandered, and you would think about your next vacation or some place you loved visiting.

    Act as if it is the very first time you have been in the meeting. What do you notice? Your only job is to observe. Let any thoughts drift away.

    Use this technique with any person, place, or situation, telling yourself it is the very first time you have seen or heard or been there. Just observe and notice. What is different? This ability to reboot your attention to see more of your environment keeps you from being complacent, distracted, smug, or stuck.

    It is easy to block out small details in your environment and your interactions when caught up in the "doing" of daily life. It is easier for emotional hijacking to occur when you are distracted. Compulsive doing can create an attitude of, "I can do it all," "I know everything there is to know," or, the opposite, "Nothing ever changes."

There is so much missed opportunity when you go through your day distracted. Bring your attention into the moment, and then learn to power up your thoughts. The more you act deliberately rather than distracted, the greater your confidence and ability to manage stress.

Remember Lynn? She started her mindfulness practice by savoring moments with her children. "I gave my daughter three seconds, looked into her eyes, told he how proud I was of her and taught her how to deep breathe. It was amazing because she calmed down and went with the busy flow in the morning. I think she was more needy when she sensed I was in a rush."

What do you do every day where you can use the three second savor and stay in the moment? Begin your mindfulness practice with this one simple practice.

Body Scan

This is a helpful practice: check in with your physical body and notice what is going on. This will make you aware of the impact of people, situations, and even food. When are you energized? Tense? Does your energy drag after certain meetings? Tension in your neck, back?

Instructions

Start with the count-of-four breathing: breathe in on a count of four, hold your breath for four, and then exhale on four. Then, breathing slower and deeper than usual, start at the top of your head and scan all the way down your body to your toes. Notice if there is any tightness, tension, or body aches. For now, simply observe what you are feeling. Ask yourself:

- Are there any emotions trying to come through the tension?
- Am I thirsty, hungry, tired, cranky?

If distracting thoughts show up, go back to the scan and just observe what you are experiencing. During the scan, for 15 seconds, you are simply observing. Being able to maintain this discipline of mindfulness will slow down your reactions and increase your awareness.

Now that you have noticed something, go back to that spot and, keeping your thoughts neutral, breathe more slowly and deeply than usual into that spot and repeat, "I release and let go."

Do this several times during the day. You will do this automatically after a few weeks of practicing this technique.

You can journal your thoughts.

The Focus Challenge

We are all familiar with natural rhythms of the seasons, the ebb and flow of the waves and the daily rhythm of day into night. We have all experienced hormonal cycles (yes, men have hormonal variations too!) and the well-known REM sleep cycle that allows for deep and restorative sleep.

Those same cycles continue during the day every 90-120 minutes, called ultradian rhythm. These cycles denote the activity-rest cycles of our body. Too often, these cycles are ignored, resulting in many of the stress related problems like overeating, mood issues, anxiety, loss of motivation, immune problems, just to name a few. The body is a self-regulating miracle and designed to self-correct when given the opportunity.

The parts of the brain the regulate the body's ability to restore itself (homeostasis) is the limbic system (also responsible for emotions) and the hypothalamus, responsible for temperature, sex drive, appetite to name a few of its functions.

Anyone who has flown through various time zones has experienced jet lag with increased fatigue and difficulty concentrating. If you have worked shift work, you have also gone through phases when you have trouble concentrating, an inability to sleep deeply and immunity to any caffeine boost. When this goes on long enough, you hit the wall with adrenal fatigue, exhaustion that is not relieved with sleep, mood problems and loss of motivation or interest, at the tip of the iceberg.

There has been tremendous research on fatigue, sleep and its impact on performance.[2] I bet you have done your own "research," having shaved off sleep time, relaxation and healthy habits to get more done. How is that working out for you?

We talked about the overload of information, the tsunami of interruptions and distractions which cause trouble with focus, memory and concentration; it also interferes with your awareness of your body's natural rhythms. When this happens during the day, it also happens at night, interrupting effective sleep. The **One-Minute Shift** will give you a way to tune into your natural energy flow, get more done and have time to spare for you.

One-Minute Shift

This one-minute activity practiced four to five times a day will transform your energy and recharge you in a surprising way!

Use your timer and set up [4-5] 2-hour intervals. Use the one-minute routine when the timer goes off.

1. Sip of water. *5 seconds*

2. Stretch. Stand up, stretch your arms over your head, then bend over and dangle. *10 seconds*

3. Use the Feelings Chart and identify how you feel. (Frustration, etc.) *15 seconds*

4. Practice deliberate breathing (You can also bring in essential oils and inhale as you breathe). *15 seconds*

5. Now bring up feelings of gratitude; inhale gratitude and exhale the frustration (or the feeling you identified). *15 seconds*

Check in. How do you feel now?

Repeat these steps for one minute. You can also extend it for five minutes which will have an even greater impact on your energy and ability to concentrate.

The 20-Minute Rule

Add this in to the one-minute shift, **once** during the day.

Engage in twenty minutes of UNINTERRUPTED time.

Turn your phone off or silence any alarms and the ringer, close the door, put up "Do Not Disturb" sign and give yourself 20 minutes of focused time to read something or complete a task. Jot down any thoughts that show up during this task; deal with them later. Resist the urge to answer texts, calls or to follow through on your thoughts. Keep a list to follow up later.

Stick to your task in front of you for 20 uninterrupted minutes. You WILL be more productive overall.

The One-Minute Shift will help you tune into the fluctuations in your concentration that occur naturally and give you the steps to refocus and restore yourself.

The Mechanism of Mindset: Awareness. Plan. Action.

Mindset is defined as a fixed mental attitude that predetermines a person's responses. This means your mindset drives your behavior. Mindset is made up of your thoughts, attitudes and choices.

Mindset is the lens through which you see the world. It should be evaluated—often. Mindset:

- Creates bias and blind spots
- Shaped by our experiences
- Can be changed (although it is difficult without awareness)
- Is a collection of habits
- Drives your actions and choices

Mindset stays flexible when you make a commitment to continual growth. Most people live in their comfort zone and rarely venture out of this unless they are forced. This is the power of transitions in life and work, planned and unplanned, that force one to see their world through a different lens.

Recently I met a colleague who shared a fantastic opportunity to train a new group of people. While he was an expert in the subject matter, he had not taught people in this industry. I asked him what his approach would be, and he said, "I am going to do what I have always done." I replied, "this is new, why would you do the same thing you have always done?" His reply, "because it worked in the past."

I believe this response is typical; however, the logic doesn't work, and the mindset is rigid. My friend chose his comfort zone over taking a risk and using an updated approach more suitable to his new audience. He stuck to an approach he had used twenty years ago. He was stuck in his blind spot.

Mindset is fueled by awareness; without it you are stuck doing the same thing you have always done.

Awareness increases your choices.

People who are self-aware have better relationships, personally and at work, they are more engaged team members, produce more and enjoy greater satisfaction. With all these benefits, why aren't more people aware? Remember, mindset creates blind spots and bias and shapes your choices. You need awareness to transform your mindset!

Start by finding out where you are now. This can be done using assessments, feedback, coaching and simple reflection. Since you are reading this book and enrolled in this program, you have chosen to grow and develop your mindset. Chapter 2 takes you through a process to identify where you are now and where you want to go.

> **Awareness is the fuel that propels you to grow.**

As an Executive Coach, I look for ways to develop my client's awareness. I use tools within Agile Lean Sigma to increase awareness of what is happening, why it is happening, and how to prevent problems and improve the outcome. This often opens managers eyes as they see the workflow mapped out and the impact of their decisions.

In my one on one sessions, we go further and explore how they, as leaders, impact the situation. We explore their inner flow and emotional effectiveness developing their self-awareness. This is the most powerful benefit of coaching and why you move further ahead, faster—because your mindset shifts from the new experience.

These tools can also be used in your personal life. In the next section, you will have four simple questions to consider, before setting up your action plan.

100-Day Action Plan

An action plan is essential to achieving results; taking the right action will get you the results you want. Every plan should include a review process. Take the time to ask yourself these questions and you will be better prepared to set up your plan.

The four questions are part of the review process; you will learn so much by exploring these answers. Now you can course correct and have the results you really want.

1. What was my objective?
2. How did I perform?
3. How did the process go? What did I learn?
4. What would make it better the next time?

These simple questions will build on your success and keep you focused on your main objective. I like to use a 100 Day roadmap to map out small steps toward your goal. Incremental change is more successful than planning big sweeping change.

Taking small steps, measuring your progress and making the necessary adjustments along the way will ensure you achieve your goals. In this world of multi-tasking, not enough of right activity gets done. Busyness replaces focus.

The 100-Day Roadmap is based on ten, ten-day increments of time. Download the map online. Start with your desired goal and break down the goal into milestones, smaller goals that when practiced consistently, will help you achieve your 100-day goal.

Your 100-Day Plan

Now, it's your turn. Create your 100-day map to activate a resilient mindset. You can download a PDF file on the membership site (details on how to access this site are included in the back of this book).

Desired Goal

_____

_____

_____

_____

Now set up a list of action items and map them out over 100 days. Check out the sample map.

Sample 100-Day Map

Goal: See the opportunity in challenges. Think positive.								
DATE	10/1	10/11	10/21	10/31	11/10	11/20	12/1	12/11
Deliberate breathing	1 min	3 min	5 min	7 min	9 min	11 min	15 min	
Monitor Inner Critic		3 days	Reframe negative self-talk			recheck		
Daily Review	x	x	Are you con-sistent?	x	x	x	x	
Exercise 15 min	x	x	x	Check-point	x	x	x	x
Track energy level					Review	Make adjust-ments		
Set up next 100 d				Review, revise				New plan

91

Do all you can;
do it the best you can—
consistently.

Emotions, Mindset, and Habits for a No-Excuses Life.

Do you make excuses for why you have not achieved your goal? Is it because of someone else? A change in your work schedule? Family demands? School? Yes, those things can impact your ability to get things done, and they change how you approach your goal. However, they should not stop you from *achieving* your goal.

Do you know the number-one predictor for success? Mindset. It is not your education, status, how much money you have, or who you know—it is how you see yourself and your attitude toward challenges. Are they opportunities? Or are they an excuse to give up?

One of the reasons I decided to author this book—and the program that accompanies it—was my struggle with mindset. Recently, I took on the role of caretaker for my husband, and I found myself feeling trapped. In turn, my thoughts become more negative, especially about my future. Every time I had an idea, a negative thought would follow with a heavy feeling of, "Why bother?" Eventually, I worked through my emotions and saw my situation as a *choice*—because of the commitment to our relationship—and I freed up my emotional reaction and my self-image.

Over the past twenty-plus years, I have had several businesses. I knew how important my mindset was after building those businesses from scratch. In this current situation of feeling trapped, it was painfully clear how much of an impact self-image and mindset has on our success.

It is human nature to not even try when you don't believe you have the skills or grit to get it done. It's also natural to think about how this achievement will impact your life: is the effort worth it?

We have trouble relating to our future self, which compounds the issue. Without an emotional connection to this "self," he or she is somewhat of a stranger. When you feel passionate about your goal, you engage your future self through an emotional connection.

Just as cortisol stimulates the fight-or-flight mechanism, oxytocin stimulates motivation. The stress reaction has a double whammy: it stimulates cortisol *and* depletes the restorative hormones like DHEA and oxytocin. Oxytocin is stimulated through heart-centered emotions like love, courage, and gratitude. When you are passionate about your goal, this engages your physiology, makes your future-self more personal, and promotes an internal commitment.

I want to share a personal story that speaks directly to this issue. When I was in graduate school, I started with thirty-five other students. Slowly, people dropped out because of sickness, family trouble, or financial issues that spread through this small group. I noticed some students returned after facing their challenge. My heart went out to one woman who had lost her mother; I was impressed by her fortitude. She told me, "I had to come back. My mother wanted me to get this degree." Her love for her mother translated into love for the process.

I went through a divorce during school after discovering my husband was cheating. I told myself I was going to complete this degree and be one of the few to move beyond the ABD phase, all but dissertation. This was the phase in the graduate process where the classes were complete, the exams were done, and all was left was the dissertation; this is where students got stuck. My motivation? Feeling rejected and struggling with self-doubt because of the relationship failure, I knew this achievement would be a turning point in my life. I could stay in this place of despair and loss, or I could move through it. I felt a burning desire to overcome any odds. I used visualization and saw myself presenting my dissertation to the committee and receiving my diploma. I surrounded my future self with love and admiration, and I pushed myself to get through whatever challenge showed up. And there were many challenges, yet to be overcome; I committed to a no excuses life.

Let's look at the emotions that underlie our thoughts and mindset. I want to add that being in a psychology program helped me to get through the roller coaster of emotions and understand what was happening.

The Black Box: Emotions are part of your survival kit.

For too many, emotions are the black box in the aircraft. You look at them only when there has been a crash or a tragedy. It is natural to have a stream of thoughts running in the background that are triggered by emotions and ignored most of the time.

We have an estimated 50,000 to 80,000 thoughts per day, and they include fears, self-doubt, and negative self-talk. The more you try to avoid or minimize the negative thoughts and emotions, the greater the impact.

To deal with these thoughts, you must acknowledge that they're there in the first place so you can dismiss them and shift into a mindset that aligns with your ultimate goals (versus getting drawn into the emotional tone).

Check out the following assumptions many hold regarding emotions:

- Emotions should be neither seen nor heard
- It is impossible to manage them, so it is best to ignore them
- Emotions get in the way of strategic decisions
- Emotions are a sign of weakness
- Emotions are not safe

"I keep my emotions in check." How many times have you said that? And how many times do you find yourself overreacting or falling flat in a conversation or at a loss for empathy?

Damasio, researcher and author on emotions, defines emotions as "complicated collections of... responses, ... [with a] regulatory role to play ... to assist the organism in maintaining life."[14] He acknowledges that emotion and reason are related; in other words, we all come equipped with a collection of emotions as part of our survival kit.

In other words, emotions are hardwired and necessary for our survival. Darwin found emotions were expressed in a similar way across cultures. Emotions *ensure* survival. The message that "one can separate one's emotions and still function well" is a myth. We are biologically hardwired to use emotional cues to make decisions and get through the day. Survival depends on the recognition of emotional cues.

The limbic system is where emotions live in the brain. About the size of a walnut, the limbic system consists of the parts of the brain that are involved in emotional memory and motivation. Structures such as the amygdala, olfactory bulb, and hippocampus (to name a few) play an important role in the expression of emotions. This region of the brain, sometimes called the "feeling" brain, sits underneath the cortex, or the "thinking brain."

Here is one time when size doesn't matter. The size of the cortex might imply power over the smaller structures of the brain; however, as we mentioned before, the amygdala is part of the survival instinct of the primitive brain and can trigger an emotional hijacking that will throw off even the smartest intellect.

The fact is, we are hardwired to feel first, and then think. These feelings can be exaggerated and inaccurate. At the very least, they may not be relevant to what is happening in the moment. Self-awareness keeps you in check and able to manage your emotions so you can stay focused on your goal. Awareness also keeps you in touch with how your behavior impacts others. Knowing the impact, you have on others will improve your influence and communication skills to motivate and inspire others.

Emotional Hijacking (The Runaway Stress Reaction)

Stress is a hardwired, primitive reaction designed as a survival instinct. When you have chronic stress and an underdeveloped ability to withstand it (resilience), there are several consequences: loss of emotional control, slower information processing, and a decrease in working memory, impacting long-range planning and creativity.

Stress triggers the amygdala—the part of the brain that monitors the environment for fear-inducing stimuli—swamping more rational thought processes. This is the fast track of the stressed response.

You are hardwired: first you feel, and then you think.

Building your capacity allows you to rationally interpret feedback from your interactions and from the environment. Stress tolerance means you operate more from the higher function of your brain (cortex) and avoid triggering the primitive survival instinct of the amygdala.

This is *focus*. This allows for systematic and methodical processing, critical thinking, and an evaluation process, making decisions better overall.

Stress tolerance *does not* mean you take whatever comes at you without flinching!

Chronic, unmanaged stress interrupts the ability to think clearly, remember things, and retrieve important data. This is hardwired physiology and the impact of too much cortisol circulating through your body. Many, in hindsight, recognize that stress contributed to decisions that were not well thought-out or to emotional reactions uncharacteristic of their usual behavior. They are left with the challenge of damage control because of their reactions and poor decisions.

How much time is wasted on repairing the fallout from hijacked reactions? Have you lost relationships because of being hijacked?

When you cannot think straight under pressure, you will undermine your best judgment, morale, and successful outcomes, adding to the stress. This problem can be prevented by learning and engaging in strategies to manage your energy.

Think about those times in your life when the pressure seemed to exceed your capacity, what types of decisions did you make? Was there any fallout from those decisions? How might the decision have been different if you had been able to think more clearly?

Emotional Awareness (Name it and Tame it)

Most people go through the day locked into a habitual pattern of reacting. It is only when you begin to question your reactions and emotions that you begin to understand what you are feeling and why.

Take a moment to reflect on the history of your emotional patterns. In reflecting, you can break through any patterns that no longer work for you. This exercise is a great introduction to your emotions and builds self-awareness.

To help you tune in and become more aware of your emotional experiences, evaluate the following questions:

Anger · Happiness · Anxiety · Fear · Sadness

1. Look at the 5 feelings above. What feeling is usually most intense for you using a 1-10 scale?

    0 _____ 10

    Feeling: _____

2. What feeling is most frequent on a 1-10 scale?

    0 _____ 10

    Feeling: _____

3. What is the typical outcome as a result of this feeling? Does it impact your relationships, job, energy levels, or motivation?

Next, we will look at each emotion individually. Take the time to reflect on these questions and journal your answers.

Anger

How do you know you are angry? What do you feel in your body?

What happens as a result of experiencing anger?

How does it affect other people?

How does it interfere with your goals?

How would you prefer to experience anger?

_____

_____

_____

Who or what flips your anger switch?

_____

_____

Anger is an important emotion. I want you to get to know your anger. When ignored, anger turns to rage, resentment, heart disease, and worse, it shuts down your ability to be happy and enjoy your life.

Remember, emotions are neither good nor bad. They are designed to inform you.

What Anger Is Telling You

Remembering that all emotions are designed to flow and inform, know that anger alerts you to set boundaries and facilitate change. That could be simply putting your hand up and saying, "Stop," when someone is attempting to force you to do something you do not want to do or talking at you and disrespecting your space.

Anger is a universal emotion that has a variety of styles of expression across different cultures, families, and genders. Women are more than likely taught to hold it in, while men are taught to express it. Some people see anger as a masculine emotion.

Most people deny their anger for a variety of reasons. When this happens, you can count on it showing up at the worst possible time. Like all emotions, anger is an internal signal to take some sort of action.

Denying your anger can increase the use of sarcasm, passive-aggressive behaviors, and other mixed signals, decreasing your ability to communicate clearly. The reflection exercise on the previous page will help you be aware of when anger shows up and its impact on you and the people around you.

We have several techniques on the online program to help you transform your anger.

Happiness

How do you know you are happy? What do you feel in your body?

What happens as a result of experiencing happiness?

How does it enhance your goal?

What would it take to experience more happiness?

_____

_____

What experiences flip your happiness switch on?

_____

_____

_____

Happiness is an individual experience. Thousands of years ago, Aristotle recognized that more than anything, people sought happiness. People seek happiness for its own sake. It can be an experience that defies words.

Defining happiness is difficult, and people often start out by saying what happiness is not. It is not having all the money or time in the world. It is doing something meaningful. It is not feeling good all the time nor is it a destination. It is fleeting, elusive, and takes time. Trying too hard gets in the way of happiness.

Happiness is on a continuum and includes feeling cheerful, satisfied, content, as well as optimistic. It is personal.

Boredom is a barrier to happiness. And boredom is telling you to stretch yourself, grow, and learn something new. Happiness is best achieved in the act of reaching for a goal and doing something you did not think you could do.

Be sure to reflect on the questions and journal your answers. The more you cultivate happiness, the less likely you will get stuck in an emotional storm.

Anxiety

How do you know you are anxious? What do you feel in your body?

_____

_____

_____

What happens as a result of experiencing anxiety?

_____

_____

_____

How does it interfere with your goal?

_____

_____

_____

What would you like to experience instead?

_____

_____

_____

Who or what flips your anxiety switch on?

_____

_____

Fear, when chronic and generalized, becomes anxiety. Anxiety arises from thoughts. It can catch you in an endless thought loop. Did I sign off on that contract? Did I forget something? What if *xyz* happens—what then? And on and on and on. Many people I talk to experience this type of endless questioning at the end of the day.

What Anxiety Is Telling You

Anxiety, when not chronic, can serve as a messenger to help you clarify a situation in your life and act.

When anxiety becomes chronic, it can be the body's way of avoiding something. Chronic anxiety shrinks your world in the effort to avoid feeling the anxiety. Phobias become a way of coping with the anxiety.

Anxiety, as part of the fear emotion, wants you to take some sort of action. Much of the anxiety people experience results from constant distractions and not being able to remember what they've done. Use your phone to create lists or download one of the many apps that will help you stay organized and focused.

Be sure to reflect on the questions and journal your answers.

Fear

How do you know you are fearful? What do you feel in your body?

_____

_____

What happens as a result of experiencing fear?

_____

_____

_____

How does it interfere with your goal?

_____

_____

_____

What would you like to experience instead?

_____

_____

_____

Who or what flips your fear switch on?

_____

_____

_____

Fear is triggered by your primitive part of the brain, the amygdala, the alarm system in your nervous system hardwired to protect us from danger. It is instinctive, and the reaction happens instantaneously. The amygdala sends the trigger to the hypothalamus, which then creates the physiological patterns for that fear. Your heartrate can go up, and you might feel a lump in your throat, tension in your neck, numbness in your hands, and any number of other physical reactions. This reaction is stored to be used over and over, when something close to this experience happens.

Fear triggers the fight-or-flight response in the stress reaction. Your amygdala is the storehouse of all your fear experiences (even those you forget) and responds immediately when it senses an experience like what has been stored. Most of the time, people are not aware of the origin of their fear and may not be consciously aware of their reaction.

Using these stress strategies presented in this program will help you overcome the instinctive pull of this primitive reaction. Fears are usually specific to a person, place, or situation and arise from feelings.

Sadness

How do you know you are sad? What do you feel in your body?

_____
_____
_____

What happens as a result of experiencing sadness?

_____
_____

How does it interfere with your goal?

_____
_____

What would you like to experience instead?

_____
_____
_____

Who or what flips your sadness switch on?

_____
_____

Sadness is not the same as depression, although it is frequently associated with it. Depression is a more complex experience. There are the clinical definitions of depression—bipolar disorder, postpartum depression, dysthymia, mild depression, atypical depression, and major depression.

Sadness is different from grief. Grief shows up in response to losses that are irretrievable. Grief can happen as a result of a physical death or the death of a dream, an opportunity, a period in your life, part of your body—any loss that is gone forever. There are stages of grief, and—as with all emotions—it is best to move through grief present and mindful to what you are experiencing.

I highly recommend having help in moving through grief because one loss will trigger other losses you have experienced, and it quickly can feel overwhelming.

What Sadness Is Telling You

Sadness, with its heaviness, the desire to withdraw, and the need to cry, is a cue you need time to reflect, review your life, and let go of things that are not working. Sadness gives you a window into what you value. This helps you understand yourself better. When you can acknowledge your own sadness, increases your ability to demonstrate empathy. By acknowledging sadness and moving through it, you develop courage and the ability to do other difficult things. Sadness is like other emotions and is designed to flow. Acknowledge it, and remind yourself, "This too shall pass."

When sadness is not acknowledged and is ignored, you can move into despair, which is a mood and lacks the natural flow built into sadness. Crying can often provide the relief needed to let go, and, with the release of tension, you can relax and begin to restore yourself. You have heard the sayings, "I just need a good cry," or, "Have a good cry, and you will feel better." This wisdom speaks to the cleansing and refreshing nature of moving through sadness.

Get to know how sadness shows up for you; reflect on the questions and journal your answers.

Fatal Emotions

We have all received some type of disappointing news. Your promotion did not come through, the raise wasn't what you expected, you lost the bid for the job, you did not get accepted into your program—the list can go on.

Disappointment is part of living life. When you do not manage those disappointments and you become discouraged, that can be fatal. Discouragement that goes unchecked destroys self-image, confidence, and expectations for the future.

Discouragement

> *Discouragement has a germ of its own, as different from trouble as arthritis is different from a stiff joint.*
>
> *- F. Scott Fitzgerald*

The dictionary definition of discouragement is "the act of making something less likely to happen." When discouragement can grow into a mood, motivation and momentum are eroded.

The erosion can be subtle. The discouragement shifts to a feeling that "things will never work out." You may try harder only to experience more disappointment, or you may give up altogether. Either way, discouragement kills drive.

When you can identify your feelings, you will be able to take the right action to shift them.

Go from Discouraged to Determined

1. **Name it:** Whenever you feel disappointment, identify it and act.

2. **Reframe it**: Identify three things that are going well for you.

3. **Claim it**: Engage the optimist in you and recognize that it is not permanent, and things will change. Denial is what makes this emotion fatal, capable of destroying your mojo.

4. **Talk about it:** (Or, write in your journal.) Find a safe person who will simply listen. At this point, talking it out helps release the heavy emotion. You can find solutions later.

5. **Help someone else**: The tendency with discouragement is to narrow your focus and think only of your problems. Get out of yourself and reach out to someone in need.

6. **Move on**: Let it go and focus on your big vision.

In addition to these steps, do something every day to manage the stressful feelings that come up. You will learn proven strategies to activate your resilience, the more you practice these, the stronger your resilience.

Let's talk about the *most* fatal emotion, one that only happens to everyone else—denial.

Denial

> *"Most men would rather deny a hard truth than face it."*
>
> — George R.R. Martin, A Game of Thrones

It is a defense mechanism we *all* use to protect ourselves from some perceived threat. Maybe there was bad news and you instinctively minimize it to get through the emergency. This temporary use of denial is helpful.

Denial becomes fatal when you use it to avoid dealing with situations that require action. Drinking too much, avoiding dealing with financial strain, avoiding your bullying coworker, or signs your teenager is using drugs, ignoring the fact you are using food to compensate for your disappointments—these are all examples of denial that is fatal.

You can deny your own behavior or that of others. Denying your own behavior shows up in chronic blaming. If you persistently accuse others of doing something wrong, chances are the problem lies with you.

Here is an example. Nancy came to me distressed and ready to quit her job: "My boss is so disorganized! And he blames me when he misplaces reports and can't find them. The piles on his desk are a disaster. But if I say anything, I risk getting yelled at. So, I am trying to accommodate him." Thinking avoiding conflict was the answer, she was creating a bigger problem for herself.

It is helpful to realize that in any interaction, both people are responsible for the outcome. Are you contributing to a situation by trying to avoid it?

When you avoid taking any action, you are denying your responsibility in the situation. If you feel like a victim and complain, "Things always happen to me," chances are you are using denial to avoid acting.

What beliefs keep you from seeing problems as they show up?

Denial allows problematic situations and health risks to continue, ultimately creating more serious issues. If you have been exposed to traumatic events or are reaching exhaustion and you continue to push yourself, the body's ability to adapt reaches its limit and you can hit the wall. It is important to address the signs of burnout long before you crash.

It is important to address issues with your staff and followers before they become a much bigger issue. When denial can operate within a culture, you turn off creativity and initiative. In a culture steeped in denial, people essentially go to sleep.

Being realistic and facing the challenge is a characteristic of strong emotional intelligence.

The value of denial is as a short-term defense mechanism.

Suggestions to Go Beyond Denial

1. Open to feedback. Before you shut out what someone tells you, consider this: is there any truth to what they are saying?

2. Get in touch with your fears. Does change threaten you? Afraid to succeed? What are your fears?

3. Talk to someone—counselor or coach. Your friends or family are not going to move you ahead. Talk with a professional.

4. Evaluate your life to date. Is it working out the way you expected, or has it fallen short? If so, in what way? Be objective. Have your beliefs held you back? What are they?

5. Journal every day. Use the Daily Review to reflect on what is working and what isn't. Keep this for a year, and you will have

a timeline review you can use to evaluate patterns of success, avoidance, progress, or resistance.

Emotional Awareness

As you can see, emotions contain important and practical information about yourself and others. Emotions guide decisions and cannot be turned off (or on) when you go to work (or come home). They are designed to flow. It is nearly impossible to experience fulfillment if you have shut down your emotional flow. It is well accepted that emotions that are not expressed can show up as disease.

Develop the habit of tuning in to identify basic feelings like anger, sadness, fear, and happiness. This reduces the chance of being hijacked emotionally and caught off-guard, because your emotions were hidden and ignored. Researchers have found that when you can name your emotion, you are less likely to overreact because of it. Having this conscious control over what you are feeling is a major step toward managing it.

Identifying and managing your emotions is critical for good relationships and work life satisfaction. If you are reactive, you miss the subtleties in communication and the opportunities to advance your goals. To avoid over or under reacting, some rely on artificial and scripted behavior to get through work scenarios; losing the opportunity to build trust and connect with others authentically. Interactions can become stale and meaningless.

Tips to increase emotional awareness:

- Keep a daily journal, note any extreme emotions;
- Begin the habit of reflection;
- Talk your feelings over with a trusted advisor;
- Practice mindfulness, slowing down your thoughts and feelings;
- Breathe slow and deep every 90 minutes, it clears your mind;

- Use the Feeling Wheel and increase your emotional vocabulary.

For too many, emotions are ignored until they show up in an over or under-reaction that causes someone else to react. Unfortunately, you cannot un-scramble an egg; damage has been done and you have lost ground in the relationship. This also negatively impacts your confidence and esteem.

As you do the reflection exercises in this book you are increasing your awareness to manage your emotions.

Drama Triangle

Drama is draining. Do you agree?

When I hear complaints about work, it is mostly about the "politics" at work: gossip, popularity contests, excessive competition, bullying, and the battle to be heard and understood drain energy faster than anything else. Work days are longer and harder with this toxic behavior contributing to low productivity and low morale.

The cost of low productivity to the organization is in the billions with staff turnover, error, risk, and poor patient outcomes. The defensive patterns of drama derail teamwork, collaboration, and destroy productivity.

Drama kills momentum.

There are three "drama" conversations that take place. Without self-awareness, this conversation becomes a vicious cycle and you end up switching roles, going from victim to persecutor. These conversations perpetuate powerlessness and avoid accountability. They are the result of an indirect style of communication.

These patterns are defense mechanisms that allow each person to stay stuck or in the status quo. Most of the time, these patterns are unconscious; they come from a set of beliefs (with emotional cues) that undermine one's self-confidence and self-image. The way out is through awareness and development of skills in emotional intelligence: assertiveness, emotional expression, impulse control and resilience.

Let's look at each conversation individually.

"Poor Me"

This conversation comes from a "Victim" persona, feelings of hopelessness and helplessness. The unconscious intent of this conversation is to block decisions and interfere with problem solving and progress moving forward. Here is an example:

"My boss never asks my opinion. I have been here longer than anyone and I am overlooked. I was told I am negative. I think everything is fine and doesn't need all these fancy programs."

This conversation needs a "Rescuer" to jump in to save the day in order to keep the cycle going.

"I Will Save the Day"

The "Rescuer" helps even when they do not want to and ends up feeling resentful. The person feels guilty when they do not help and experiences positive self-worth by helping others. This cycle enables failure rather than accountability. It blocks empowerment and ownership.

The rescuer steps in to help the victim, except sometime the victim doesn't' want to be saved and is just looking to blame someone.

"Mary was giving her usual negative feedback when a coworker laid into her for being so negative. I could see the hurt on her face, so I stepped in. I wanted to save the day. Instead I ended up being the bad guy and was told it was none of my business."

It is best to leave the rescuing for the fairy tales. In real life, find a way to have an open and direct conversation about the issues.

"It's Your Fault"

This cycle of destructive communication starts with the blaming, shaming, and criticism from a "Persecutor." Despite the confrontational tone of this conversation, this person is coming from a powerless position, as are the other two.

The Persecutor can show up an any level of the organization, however, it is frequently coming from a manager or supervisor. This is what happened with Nancy. Her boss yelled at her for misplacing the folders, when it was his own disorganization. She played the 'victim' and avoided any conversation, while he was a perfect 'persecutor.'

Let's look at how a healthy interaction could go:

Boss, angry: "Nancy, you have misplaced my folders."

Nancy: "I placed them on your desk, on one of the piles you told me to put it on."

Boss, scowling: "How am I supposed to find anything on this desk."

Nancy: "I can help you set up a file system we both can use so you do not have to yell at me when you can't find something."

Nancy stepped up and confronted her boss in a respectful way. This gave him the opportunity to think the situation through and realized, he had told her where to put the folders. Nancy then can come in and instead of "rescuing" the situation, she is problem solving in a way where both people are accountable.

Nancy could have left out her accusation that her boss "yelled" at her; however, she chose to be direct, letting him know how she perceives him.

The motivation behind these three roles is to avoid expressing needs and or wishes directly. By relying on these defenses, you avoid developing the skills needed to leverage conflict and deal with tough conversations.

Next, take the Drama Quiz and see where you might show up in these three roles.

Drama Self-check

Read through the questions. Answer using a 1 to 10 scale with 10 being "All the time," and 1 being "Rarely." Keep in mind, just about everyone does some of this some of the time.

Your goal is to increase your awareness of your communication style. Be honest in your assessment. It's important to understand your underlying feelings, like powerlessness or anger, that may be the source of this communications style.

1 2 3 4 5 6 7 8 9 10

Rarely   All the Time

1. Do you provide unsolicited advice?
2. Do you jump to help even when not asked?
3. Do you compromise to avoid conflict and feel resentful or withdraw from the process?
4. Do you use intimidation to get your way?
5. Are you impatient when things do not go your way?
6. Do you take feedback as a personal attack?
7. Do you feel like you are the only one committed to the project and get frustrated with others?
8. Do you withhold your feelings or opinions because you feel like they won't matter?

Your Score: _____

The higher your score, the greater the chance you are engaging in the drama roles of victim, rescuer, or persecutor. What stood out to you as you went through the questions?

What will you do differently?

5 Destructive Divas

Have you ever called in "sick" (of your coworkers)? I remember, as a new nurse, my so called "preceptor" used her role to constantly criticize me. I did not want to confront her, so I called in sick!

In this section, I have laid out five different roles people play at work that disrupt productivity and morale.

Do you work with any of them? Have you been like any of them? If so, don't beat yourself up! What matters now is that you begin to identify any behaviors that may be sabotaging your success.

1. Drama Diva

Using words like *everything, always, never*, and *making mountains out of molehills*, this diva is determined to be noticed and get attention. Emotions really are our GPS (guidance for professional success); however, Drama Divas use their emotions like the siren on emergency vehicles, lights flashing and alarms blasting. You cannot miss hearing or seeing this person. The problem with this diva is even if the issue is relevant, this person is often discounted because the drama overrides the ability to tune in and track with this person.

2. Detached Diva

This individual is distant and aloof and does not interact or join in any unit activities. There could be a hidden layer of resentment or fear of rejection setting up a barrier to getting to know anyone. The detachment can be interpreted by others as indifference, creating gossip or judgement toward that person. This is a problem because when help is needed, this person is so used to working alone that they do not notice when someone needs help. Their standoffishness also keeps others from asking them for help. This breaks up the cohesiveness of the team.

3. No-Way Diva

This individual says "no" or complains about everything before they even know what it is. This individual makes it tough to ask for help because you know they will say "no." This person finds ways to get out of doing work and is happy to let other people do the jobs they do not want to do. They get away with it because no one wants to confront them. This diva will intimidate their coworkers when necessary.

4. BFF Diva

This diva is friendly to a fault—interested in hearing all about your weekend, plans for vacation, and even what you are making for dinner, but not interested in doing any work. While friendly, this diva does not like to be told they are slacking and will claim they are building team spirit and keeping the morale up.

5. Super Diva

This diva is the Superhero of the unit, wanting to be all things to all people. Not able to say "no," this individual takes on tasks and assignments wanting to do everything themselves. This martyrdom usually comes with some resentment and feeling like they are better than everyone else. This diva has issues with control and may feel like they must prove something to others. It creates resentment and tension in the team as others feel like they need to compete. This person is also more likely to burn out.

Are you a Diva? Shift to Delightful

1. Learn to laugh at yourself and recognize we are all growing, learning, and developing personally and professionally.

2. Spend some quiet time and reflect on what you need. How do you feel most heard and validated? Set up a plan to get it.

3. Before you express yourself verbally, write it out. This will diffuse any intense emotions and help you express yourself more rationally.

4. Recognize that working together as part of a team is what makes work more enjoyable and less stressful. Be a part of the solution.

5. Breathe deeply for five seconds before you say anything.

6. Recognize that your behavior has an impact on everyone in your department. Check in with yourself and ask the question, "Would I want to work with someone like me?"

Habits

Think about your day. What do you when you wake up? If you run, how do you tie your shoes? What are the habits that drive you? Researchers say 40% (and maybe more) of what you do during the day is a habit. And 90% of what we do is directed by our unconscious mind and happens automatically. What this means is that you are forming habits without even realizing it.

Driving to work, you automatically turn the wheel, turn on the blinker, and handle the car, without having to think about it. This saves energy; it is your brain being efficient. You may also be stopping in the cafeteria and picking up a brownie, automatically, because it picks you up in the late morning. This is a new habit you have developed, without realizing it.

In this section, we are going to explore how habits are formed and how to change habits that get in the way of you being your best.

Our nervous system—especially our brain—loves to keep us safe and conserve energy. Habits are how our nervous system functions. For now, rather than thinking they are good or bad, look at habits as ways of simplifying how you get things done. Imagine if you had to think about every activity in your day from scratch? You would be exhausted by 9 a.m.

Brushing your teeth, making coffee, lacing up your running shoes, and so many other habits help you throughout your day. And many of these habits were probably started because they initially helped you achieve a goal, but now they are interfering with your daily performance.

Many habits aren't even labeled as "bad" by most people but can be interfering with you being your best. Could your habit of complaining when you are given a new assignment be the reason your boss overlooked you for the promotion? Complaining slows your progress, interferes with your internal creativity, and leaves your boss with the wrong impression. Yet, you may not notice it or realize it's a habit.

To identify your habits, think about any outcomes you do not regularly achieve. Then, walk back and look closely at your routines or thought processes. Ask yourself, *Does this habit advance my progress or keep me going in circles?* Which habits do you want to change because they are interfering with making progress?

Take a deep breath and think through your day, from the time you get up in the morning to the time you go to bed. Draw a timeline of your habits. Which habits create a chain reaction that may be sabotaging your best performance?

Jess shared her typical day with me at a training I did at her workplace. She said she wanted to stop drinking so much coffee. At first glance, it seemed logical to think, just cut back on the coffee. Let's take a deeper look at what is happening.

"I get up early and start my coffee fix. I need it because I never feel rested when I wake up. I get home from work and get dinner for my family and that leaves little time for myself. I end up staying up late scrolling through social media! And by then it is late. I am not getting the sleep I need."

My suggestion to Jess is to change the nighttime routine of scrolling through social media. We agreed she would give herself thirty minutes on social media, using a timer, while the kids are watching a TV program. This way she can begin a relaxing routine at night to get ready for bed. This is a start to stopping the excessive coffee habit. With better rest, she can begin her day with water to naturally energize her.

Awareness of what you are doing and why will serve you with any habit you want to break and then rebuild. Once you understand what happens in a habit—its structure—you can make those incremental changes that add up to a big change.

Increasing your awareness and mindfulness is especially helpful; most of your daily activity is driven by your automatic mind, your unconscious.

For example, imagine walking to a meeting. You skipped lunch and are hungry, the reports came back with less than stellar numbers, you are disappointed, you remember how your boss reacted the last time this happened, and the noise coming from the construction outside is louder than you recall. You see Mary from the marketing department. You met her last week in a meeting, but you are so distracted by the overload of stimuli that you do not stop to chat. You grimace as you pass her in the hallway. Mary thinks it is because of her.

You are not aware of your grimace, so you do not understand why Mary now avoids you. Your automatic mind was in charge, making associations as you walked down the hall, distracted by this internal noise.

The more aware of your associations you are, the easier it is to tease out the cues for your habits.

Habits form because the brain wants to save energy; its instinct is to turn everything into a habit. But because survival is paramount to the primitive brain, it recognizes that it cannot lose attention and miss something that may threaten it. To manage this initial uncertainty, the brain will establish a cue that lets it know which pattern to use.

In my private practice, I used hypnotherapy to help smokers quit. When identifying cravings, a very difficult craving to stop was smoking in the car. The cue was putting the key in the ignition: that told their brain it was time to light up. The cue for any craving alerts your nervous system for a specific routine and reward loop. The reward tells your brain to remember this routine.

The structure of a habit is the cue, routine, and reward. The more you engage in this habit, the more automatic it becomes, until you begin to anticipate and crave the habit. To change the habit, you want to change the routine—the response to the cue.

You also want to understand what the cue is and why it is necessary. Let's go back to the example of complaining every time you are given a new assignment. The cue is the anxiety you feel when your boss gives you something new to do. When you slow everything down, you recognize the thoughts running through your mind: "Do I have the time?" "Can I do this?" This created anxiety and the complaining reduces the anxiety you felt, which is the reward.

To change the habit, change the routine. Instead of complaining, which interferes with your performance and gives your boss the wrong impression about you, you can ask questions about what the assignment entails. This will give you the same reward—relief from anxiety—but better outcomes in the long run.

This change in habit also helps you feel better about yourself, increases your learning on the job, and will open opportunity as people around you see a shift in attitude. What mental or emotional habits are obstructing your success?

Take this as a challenge to shift out of autopilot—going through the motions and engaging in old and familiar routines because your brain wants to be safe and efficient—and shift into living a no-excuses life.

Infrastructure Habits (The Habits to Build On)

You know now that most of your day-to-day activity is designed around habits—some good and others not so much. And you have probably tried to change your habits many different times. Did you know that certain habits provide a structure for other habits to thrive—or not?

Remember Jess? Getting adequate sleep is a foundational habit. When this need is not met, it is easy to develop habits that compensate, i.e., scrolling through social media late into the night.

Think about your day: what habits give you the most energy and vitality to perform at your best?

For most people, sleep habits, diet, drinking enough water to energize you, exercise, and some type of prayer, meditation, or stress relief are the "Infrastructure Habits" that help you build on other great habits and a power mindset.

Consider this: when you are well rested, you wake up earlier, have more time in your day, are more energized, and are probably happier. This builds your confidence and feeds the desire to keep your momentum going.

What happens when you do not sleep well? You compensate for the lack of energy and focus and may use caffeine to overstimulate, which has consequences, like increased irritability and sleep interference. The vicious cycle is born.

In your workbook, I have a Daily Monitor you can use for these habits, along with space for you to write in those habits that keep you well fueled and focused. The main goal of these exercises is to increase your awareness. Learn more about yourself—what increases your motivation and what decreases it. There are days when the loss of motivation is subtle, and without the habit of reflection, you will miss the trigger that derails you.

Infrastructure Habits Include:

- Sleep habits
- Food/fuel (what type of food plan best serves your energy?)
- Water/hydration

- Exercise/movement
- Inspiration/spiritual food
- Financial/savings goals

Evaluate your day and see how well you are tuned in to these basic habits. Use your workbook and the tools we have in this section to monitor these habits. You may find that stabilizing these habits will help you make changes in other areas easier.

I have seen the desire to continue some destructive habits disappear once you stabilize these foundational habits. The cue can disappear for those behaviors that are compensating for one of the infrastructure habits that's lacking.

This brings us to the Mindset Habits that are foundational to a power mindset and living a no-excuses life.

Mindset Habits

Henry Ford said it best: "Whether you think you can, or you think you can't, you are right."

Mindset is everything. If you do not believe you can do something, you are not going to try. This is even true in relationships. Research has found that when one partner puts demands on the other, if that partner does not feel they can meet those demands, they don't even try.

Think about your own life. Is there an area you would like to improve, but your mindset is negative? How is that working out?

What mindset habits do you want to build?

- **Optimism**. Yes, I've mentioned the Optimism Bias. However, being optimistic means, you recognize your strengths and keep going, despite the challenge in front of you. Being optimistic includes confidence in your ability to meet challenges.

- **Coachability.** This is your willingness to learn times your willingness to act. Research shows those who act within 24 hours end up achieving more.

- **Flexible.** Change is the new normal; the rate and pace of change today is unprecedented. When you can quickly reevaluate your options and are open to change, you will win—every time. The person with the greatest flexibility in their behavior controls the outcome in relationships or negotiation.

- **Focus.** Your attention is your greatest asset. Distractions drain your energy and destroy the ability to finish tasks and do a job well. Having a focused mindset helps you concentrate and prioritize the most important tasks.

These mindset habits will make it easier to develop the habits you want.

From Autopilot to Power Mindset

Your primitive brain is like the thermostat in your home. Once you set it at a certain temperature, it turns the system on and off to keep the temperature stable. Unfortunately, this safe and efficient system will not produce peak performance, innovation, or inspiration. Its job is to keep you safe and to conserve energy. It is up to you to power up your brain and go beyond the autopilot settings.

Consider the tools you are learning in this program as your upgrade for your thinking.

Your brain is an amazing structure: 86 billion neurons, communicating with your entire body through synaptic connections and a host of biochemicals that travel throughout, creating sensations, emotions, and impressions and stimulating critical functions for your health and wellbeing. Through research on neuroplasticity, we now know that your brain is plastic. When given the opportunity, your brain learns and adapts. Your brain builds neural pathways and sets up default modes of responding.

Neuroplasticity demonstrates that the brain is capable of learning new ways of doing things—provided you try new ways to do things. If you always respond the way you have always responded, you will always react the way you have always reacted. This routine sets up a default pathway in your brain, making it easier to respond that way all the time.

Do you complain more than you don't? Are you easily angered or feel resentful? Do you look for shortcuts, even when you know going through the process as expected will yield better results? Habits of mind—as well as physical habits like smoking, drinking, or using substances to alter your mood—can all be changed by exploring your habits and changing your routines. Go to the online program and workbook for exercises and audio resources.

You can power up your mindset using these suggestions by increasing the following in your day:

- **Gratitude** changes the way your brain works and stimulates a different set of hormones that broadens your perspective.

- **Curiosity** increases the firing of different neurons. The brain loves novelty and will open new opportunity for your thought processes.

- **Physical exercise** stimulates your thinking. In just 15 minutes per day, you can increase your productivity by over 25%.

You were born with a brain. It is up to you to engage all its amazing resources and run it with a resilient mindset.

You, 2.0: A Better, Rewired Version of You

Let me introduce you to Matt, a new physician who started work in an Internal Medicine practice right out of school. "I graduated from medical school and should be happy, instead my relationship is falling apart, and I am not sure about my future in medicine."

His most recent performance review shocked him because it was so poor. A high achiever his whole life, he did not understand how he could have such a poor review. He allowed that review to define his future and his capacity.

He got through medical school by spending his time studying, sacrificing any social life. He had always wanted to be a physician. Once he graduated, he told himself he shouldn't have to work 20-hour days. He could finally enjoy a relationship and have a life outside of work.

He took a job right out of school without giving any thought to what he really enjoyed about being a physician: working with his hands and doing the type of work common in an Urgent Care or Emergency Room. He was drained working with chronically ill patients.

He had gotten through medical school by pushing himself; he knew he could get through because there was an end to school. He did not take the time to think more deeply about what he liked, what he didn't, and what would bring him the most joy. He had never considered his capacity for relationships, interaction, or the self-awareness needed to be successful in these areas.

Transitions force us to get to know more about ourselves because they bring about changes, challenging us to consider our capacity.

This was very true for Mary Jean. She was recently widowed and decided to move to a resort town. In her grief, she made the commitment to open her capacity for adventure and new experiences. She missed her husband, but despite the loss, she knew there was more life in her and she did not want to waste any time without exploring this potential.

Contrast this with Joelle, who opened her dream business only to realize she did not have the skills to manage the details and found herself working long days with very little to show for it. She closed the craft business after 12 months. She decided she would never pick up a craft again, despite previously loving it.

At some point in life, we are all challenged to get to know ourselves and learn about our hidden potential, both strengths and areas that need improvement. Transition and struggle bring out hidden potential (capacity). It can also shut it down. Your mindset determines how you approach the challenge.

Do you go for it—or not?

Now that you have the tools to change your reaction to stress and you know how to build habits that support your goals, let's look at your confidence and upgrade to a better version of you.

Confidence

The dictionary defines confidence as:

- the state of feeling certain about the truth of something
- a feeling of self-assurance arising from one's appreciation of one's own abilities or qualities

The word "confidence" comes from a Latin word meaning "with faith," and "faith" is belief in things unseen. This means you have confidence in your ability to show up and do your best. Your ability to perform at an expert level comes from your confidence. When you believe in yourself, you will make the effort to practice, learn, and grow your expertise.

In my practice, I have been surprised by the number of very talented people who have the expertise yet lack the authentic confidence in their essence—the ability to show up. This relates to early conditioning and outdated beliefs about themselves from childhood.

Congratulations to you on your willingness to challenge your own belief system and break down barriers to be the best version of you.

Confidence is more about how you approach challenges than a set of skills or competencies. And confidence may be even more important than competencies. Here is where it gets interesting!

It can be difficult to find confidence in action. We see *bravado* every day in the workplace—an outward, showy bluster that can give away an underlying insecurity when you tune in to that person's body language. Despite the loud claims of confidence, there may be a shrill voice and lack of eye contact. How do you respond to someone like this? Does your "BS" detector pick up on this fake confidence?

Faking confidence or being overconfident eventually backfires. Confidence drives us to keep going, ultimately developing skills and abilities. When you are overconfident, you do not seek to develop your skills, and you fall prey to a bias that prevents you from learning and growing.

Men and women experience confidence differently. Researchers have shown that men generally *demonstrate* more confidence than women even when they are *less* qualified!

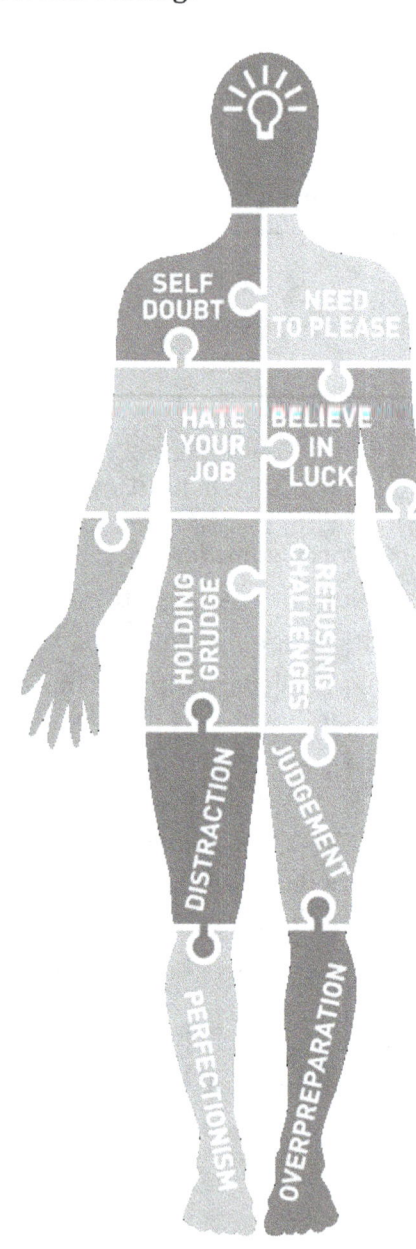

Women often feel a certain level of confidence is "presumptuous," whereas men will easily see themselves achieving higher levels of success. Women run the risk of the "Imposter Syndrome," a form of self-doubt despite obvious examples of success. Women seem to think they must constantly prove their abilities.

Women are more likely to attribute their success to luck, how they look, or something outside of themselves, rather than own their skills and abilities. This difference in self-confidence is well noted in many of the recent books on women and leadership. Women tend to have lower expectations for themselves compared to men. This impacts your confidence. It is a mindset of self-doubt.

To what do you attribute your success?

a. Lucky breaks
b. Your appearance
c. Your skills and expertise
d. Who you know

What more might you achieve if you lost your self-doubt?

Own Your Confidence: Power Pose

Confidence lives as much in your body as it does as a state of mind. How you stand, sit, and hold your head and shoulders will help to engage feelings of confidence—or not. This is the phenomenon of state-dependent memory. You can recreate a feeling by recreating the "state" in which you experienced that feeling. When you sit with slumped shoulders, frowning, you will more likely feel distress or sadness because of past experiences of those feelings.

Similarly, feelings of confidence can be recreated when you remember your posture, facial expressions, and other body movements and then recreate that stance. This cues in the internal state of confidence.

How you sit and move may impact how you feel more than how you think. Here lies the power of the pose. Changing how you stand (or sit) changes how you feel and what you think about yourself. Let's try it.

Think about a time when you felt confident. How did you experience this in your body? Recreate this experience now and practice it. Hold that pose for one minute. Breathe with purpose, more slowly and deeply than usual.

Write out how you felt after engaging in this pose:

_____
_____
_____

This can be your power pose. Use visualization to see and feel yourself as confident as you assume this pose. Breathe more slowly and deeply than usual. Then send yourself love and appreciation for your courage and willingness to move ahead. Do this for three minutes. Notice how you feel when you assume the pose?

Be more aware of your body language and change the actions that are whittling away at your confidence.

Suggestion:

1. Use the lavender essential oil and breathe in deeply, inhaling the oil right from the bottle.

2. Breathe deliberately

3. Stand in your pose and feel the confidence surging through your entire body.

Confidence Killers

It's easier to talk about what kills your confidence than how to achieve it. Look at the following chart, and jot down examples of when you were guilty of these.

What do you engage in most often?

Over preparing	
Self-doubt	
Need to please	
Perfectionism	
Over-belief in luck	
Distraction	
Self-criticism	
Judgment	
Refusing a challenge	
Holding a grudge	

Your Inner Critic

Most people I talk to have an inner critic, that voice that criticizes or makes you feel small. No one was born with one. It is the result of early experiences, school and other institutions that shape our view of the world.

Do you have "you should," "why didn't you," how could you" running in the background of your mind, critiquing everything you do?

How we talk to ourselves sets the tone for our self-image and confidence. As a human being, through our self-awareness, we have the capacity to define who we are and attach a value to that identity. The Inner Critic robs you of potential and capacity.

The Inner Critic usually originates in early childhood and can result from overly critical parents; a cold, harsh attitude; increased fear; and even neglect.

Review the following questions. Your answers will be an indicator of where your Inner Critic may have come from:

1. My parents were inconsistent. I never knew what might set them off.   YES   NO

2. My parents were critical. I never felt like I could do enough.   YES   NO

3. My parents were fearful and would try to scare me out of any activity.   YES   NO

4. There was a lot of anger and then silence in my house growing up.   YES   NO

As human beings, we have great capacity for judgment—and this is a good thing when we want to evaluate right from wrong, good from bad, what color we like, foods we prefer, movies we want to watch, and the list goes on and on. The problem is, this ability extends to the Inner Critic, who has infinite opportunities to critique your every move unless you rein in the voice inside your head.

Your workbook and online program have a variety of exercises to change your relationship with your Inner Critic. I highly recommend them. It does not take long to silence this critic. The cost to your everyday success and long-term opportunity is huge when you go through your day rejecting parts of yourself.

Why Do You Listen to the Critic?

We all have basic needs and want to feel:

1. Accepted
2. Safe
3. Competent
4. Okay with ourselves

Those with a secure sense of confidence will meet these needs through their internal sense of control over themselves and their environment. Those without confidence or a secure self-esteem have more anxiety, learned helplessness, and insecurity and rely on the Critic to keep them in line or to feel safe.

This works through a cycle of reinforcement: without awareness of the Critic, you may not recognize the chain of events. You may feel anxiety related to some activity or interaction, and instead of addressing the anxiety, because it is outside your awareness, the Critic pipes up and begins to put down the situation ("an idiot could do this") or the person ("they are never satisfied"), and your anxiety is lessened. This becomes your strategy for dealing with anxiety.

Silence Your Critic

That was so stupid ... I will never get that job ... What was I thinking? If I weren't so lazy ... He is so much stronger than I am ... Why can't I ...?

The Critic doesn't always say something. It also shows up in raw emotions, split-second impressions, or flashes of memories that bring up feelings of not being good enough. One of my clients told me, "Sometimes, I feel like everything I have done is worthless. It is a huge knot in my stomach."

Awareness of your inner life is the most effective weapon against your Critic and any other negative habit you want to change. We are going to address habits in the next chapter. For now, we'll look at ways to bring your self-talk into the light.

Keep a log of your self-talk (see the following example). Yes, it might be uncomfortable, but I can assure you, the discomfort won't last long. As you finally shift your criticism to helpful dialogue, relief will replace this temporary uneasiness. Be sure to check into the online program and listen to the audio entitled, "Reframing Self-Talk."

Date/ Time	Criticism	Activity	What did I avoid?	How did I feel?
1/3, 7:15am	I am so stupid	Took the wrong exit	Missed my early meeting	Relieved

When keeping your journal, be especially alert to times when:

- You feel anxiety (i.e., around certain people)
- When you might have to take a risk (i.e., speak to a group of people)
- Situations in which you have a history of failure (i.e., working with a competitive colleague)
- Situations with disapproving people (i.e., parents, boss)
- Situations with authority figures (i.e., board meetings)
- You interact with people to whom you feel an attraction

Think of other times that you feel dread, anxiety, or otherwise want to avoid. Tune into your self-talk, and keep the journal. Go through the chart.

It is not enough to just think about it. Writing it out will help you move through this much faster.

Perfectionism

Perfectionism is on the rise. A recent study has found it equally affects men and women.[9] Researchers went on to say that perfectionism has long-term consequences with an increased risk of burnout. Living in this "always-on" world with endless social media portrayals of perfect lives only adds to the pressure to appear perfect.

Rachel came to me because her life was unraveling:

> I have always held myself to high standards. I wanted to be the perfect wife and mother. I had to always look good, keep my weight down, and turn in the best work. I used to think being a perfectionist was my secret weapon. It kept me striving to do better—until I crashed.
>
> It stopped working. Or maybe I could not keep up the façade anymore. I knew I was not perfect and never would be. I felt depressed and anxious and like nothing was working. I ping-ponged between always and never.
>
> I get so angry when my husband cannot pack a healthy lunch for the kids. I think 'bout this all day. Then, I end up making a mistake at work . . . I decided to get help and end this vicious cycle.

Very often, perfectionists hold back because they do not feel ready and they do not take risks. It is important to learn the difference between being a perfectionist and wanting to be your very best. I understand this as a recovering perfectionist.

Growing up in a "never enough" household, I kept trying harder and harder to get the approval I desperately wanted. This continued into my adult life, where it seemed like my perfectionism was paying off. After all, I was overachieving, getting promoted, and earning more money—what's not to love about that?

Eventually, like Rachel, this striving stopped producing relief from the anxiety. Just like a drug, I built up an immunity, and I had to learn to love and approve of myself. Now, when I work hard and continue to push myself, I know it is because I want to stand out and be the best. I do not have the emptiness that used to drive my ambition.

Perfectionism is a definite confidence killer. Are you waiting for the *right* moment to go for it?

Does this sound familiar? "I will go for it when I . . ."

- Lose weight
- Get the promotion
- Finish school
- Send my children to school
- Get married
- Get divorced

And there are so many other excuses that can be used to delay action.

Maybe you are waiting for *permission*? Is there someone who is depending on you, and you are hoping they will tell you it's okay to go for it? If you are looking for a sign, here it is! Go for it!

Perfectionism is the result of early conditioning, like how the Inner Critic was born. You internalize criticism, finding fault and using it to push yourself to be better.

So, what's wrong with having high standards?

Absolutely nothing. In fact, having high standards increases performance. Perfectionism is the opposite of high standards; it is punishment for never being good enough. When you seek to master your skills, there are times you fail, make mistakes, and learn from those situations. In that case, you revise your approach and try something a different way.

Perfectionism is driven by fear. And when fear is your motivation, there is an inner belief that you really are not good enough. This can cause you to stop trying, play it safe, or procrastinate. You might also work yourself so hard, you lose any enjoyment in the process. The pursuit becomes a chore and is meaningless.

Perfectionism has been shown to lead to other destructive behaviors like eating disorders. It can also lead to anxiety, depression, and suicidal tendencies.

It is time to transform perfectionism into an approach that supports an inner belief that is positive and affirming. This doesn't mean you lose your drive or your high standards. You can still work hard toward your goal. Just know this: it is far more powerful to work toward your goal feeling confident you can get there.

It is time to stop confusing compulsive doing with progress, work with accomplishment, and people pleasing with your value.

Pressure at work can contribute to the feeling, "If I work harder or longer, I will be valued." The fast pace and incessant demands of work can trigger perfectionistic behaviors with a helpless, hopeless undertone that can lead to feelings of depression.

Your awareness of why you are working so hard will help you distinguish sacrifice and choice. I remember talking with a former SEAL and asking him about the sacrifices he made during the grueling training process. His response was, "They weren't sacrifices. I made a choice to be a member of the team and chose to follow through."

Perfectionism can show when you require perfection from your children, your spouse, or your coworkers. This damages relationships and feeds the inner belief that often drives perfectionism: that you are not lovable.

When one's inner definition of self is grounded in fear, coping skills can be limited. The tendency may be to avoid your problems as a way of coping. You may believe you cannot cope in an acceptable way, and you may even tell yourself, "I should not be having this problem with everything I know."

Decide to be more accepting. Stick with this program; we can help you move beyond this confidence killer. Check out the Perfectionism Quiz in the online program. It will give you specific behaviors to look out for.

Stinkin' Thinkin' (Thinking Habits That Sabotage You)

It's natural to have a stream of thoughts running in the background of your mind. It is estimated we have between 50,000 and 80,000 thoughts per day, many of which are fears, self-doubt, and negative self-talk. And the more you ignore or avoid the negative thoughts and emotions, the greater the surprise when they show up.

The way to deal with these thoughts is to be aware of them, acknowledge them in a mindful way, and take some type of action to realign your thoughts with your intended goal (versus getting drawn into the raw emotional energy).

The following are thinking habits that undermine the moment and your capacity.

Never say never.

Overgeneralizing is focusing on one observation and not bothering to compare it to more facts to see if it's actually true. You can easily jump to conclusions when you are used to underestimating your value and overestimating your weaknesses.

If "never," "always," "everyone", and "all" are words you use, you are caught in the habit of overgeneralizing. Just because something happened one time doesn't make it true all the time.

Jesse was incredibly shy, which got worse after he gave a speech at his brother's wedding and forgot part of his speech. He concluded: "I knew right then I would never get in front of people. I felt so embarrassed and sick to my stomach." His conclusion was based on emotions that came up during his speech when he forgot the words.

The next time you find yourself overgeneralizing, challenge the self-talk. Ask for the evidence and write down your observations. We will be dealing with the emotional undertones in the next section.

"It must be my fault."

Do you tend to take responsibility for everything that happens? This pattern of thinking can happen when you do not process your emotions and resort to labeling yourself as the problem instead.

Recently, a client of mine came in to work on a Monday to find out the computer network had been hacked. She immediately cringed, remembering she had come in over the weekend. Without knowing the facts, she felt responsible, thinking she must have done something to cause the situation. "Maybe I logged out wrong?" she mumbled under her breath before feeling like a total failure and hiding out in her office the rest of the day.

The computer hack had nothing to do with her, and had she listened to the IT Director, she would have learned this was part of a broader cyber issue. "It was hard for me to approach the director, I felt responsible and did not want to get blamed."

Feeling like everything is your responsibility has shades of victim and martyrdom built into this destructive habit. This destructive thought pattern short circuits your ability to learn from what is happening around you because you are taking the blame.

Black-or-white thinking.

When you are stuck in either-or thinking, you lose sight of the many possible variations. If everyone who yells is an out-of-control person, you may choose to never yell, bottling up all your anger—or you run the risk of your Critic labeling *you* as out of control.

We have an infinite ability to judge; this is one of the strengths of our brain, yet it requires us to be aware of the emotional undertones that go with the judgement.

Focusing on the negative: filtering.

Do you hear only the negative? I remember giving a speech early in my career. I had never spoken to 400 people before, and I was nervous.

Afterward, many people came up to me and commented on how much they enjoyed the talk.

But one of the women I knew did not come up to me and instead walked out of the room without saying anything. I remember feeling like I must have failed in my delivery. What I did not know until later was that she had received an urgent text and needed to get back to the office.

Later that day, I remember realizing every single person could have given me a thumbs up, but until I approved of my delivery, there would never be enough praise. Criticism must be balanced with praise. If you did not learn this growing up, it is time to learn this now.

You are wasting your capacity and potential believing you do not have what it takes or that you will *never* achieve your goal. Time is of the essence; decide to shift this destructive habit.

Let's talk about the conscious unconscious mind. It will shed some light on what is happening with your Critic and these destructive habits.

I must "feel" like it in order to do it.

Do you put off starting something because you just don't feel like doing it? Of course, we all have. This often happens with exercise; it gets put off because one doesn't feel like exercising.

What do you put off because you do not feel like it?

Feelings can be very strong, and thoughts accompany those feelings that end up distracting you from your commitment. Let's stay you want to exercise 20 minutes a day because you know it energizes you. But one day, work is too hectic, and you do not have your usual inspiration to exercise, so you put it off. This sets up a pattern and an easy out the next time you come home and do not "feel like it."

This plays out in all types of activities. Let's say you are in sales and need to follow up with your prospect, but you just "don't feel like it." Sales professionals know that the success is in the follow through. Or perhaps you need to have a difficult conversation with an employee, but "you don't feel like it," so you put it off, and now the conversation is no longer relevant. You never have it, and the relationship suffers.

You Are Like the Titanic

The Titanic was the most amazing ship of its day. It was built as a luxury liner and thought to be unsinkable. It ended up sinking on its maiden voyage. The ship's hull was pierced by an iceberg they did not see.

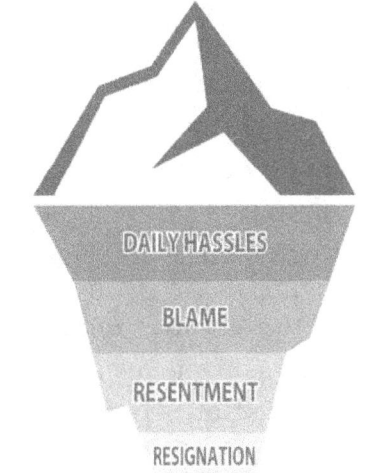

This could be a metaphor for your life when you experience an unexpected setback. The iceberg is your conscious unconscious mind. Most of the iceberg is under the water and out of sight. This is your unconscious influence on the top of the iceberg.

Your conscious mind is the part of the iceberg above the water, the mind activity is what you can see. Most thinking is unconscious influencing the conscious activity of analysis and critical thinking.

Most of the activity of your mind happens "under the water," so to speak—outside of conscious awareness. We have all been caught off guard by the "iceberg" of unconscious activity.

The unconscious makes up an estimated 95% of the activity of your mind. Fortunately, critical functions for survival like breathing, heart rate, immune activities, and many other biochemical functions take place without us thinking about it.

The unconscious mind functions much differently than our conscious mind. Everything we do and experience is stored in our unconscious. The conscious mind fatigues easily and is limited in performance capacity, which is why we have a seven-digit phone number (about as much as the conscious mind can remember).

The unconscious mind is very literal, does not recognize negatives, and is very eager to please. If I want to stop eating sugar, the usual reaction is to focus on *not* eating sugar, but in that situation, your unconscious will only focus on eating sugar. Therefore, you want to frame any of your affirmations or statements in the positive.

Your mind believes every word you tell it. Research has demonstrated the immune system's sensitivity to negative and depressing thoughts compared to positive thoughts. The mind may not be considered part of the physical body, but we now know thoughts can influence the function of the cells.[3]

Your unconscious mind runs on symbols and emotions. The limbic system, a primitive part of the brain, is instinctive and operates outside your conscious control. It responds to events, secreting a variety of neurochemicals that match the emotional experience. This part of your brain enriches this experience with an emotional imprint. This imprint gets triggered repeatedly when similar experiences happen.

Awareness is a superpower.

When you can ask yourself, "What is going on? What am I feeling, and where is this coming from?" you will break through bias and mindset distortions.

The limbic system also plays a role in long-term memory; you remember events that have made an impact on you much more easily. Your emotions are part of your survival toolkit and cannot be switched on or off. Your limbic system and your thinking brain work together to form explicit memories. This type of memory blends the information you have learned with emotions to create an experience. This deepens your knowledge and broadens your perspective.

The limbic system helps form our belief system about situations, life, and ourselves due to the emotional imprint on the experience. The more this experience (emotional imprint) happens, the more hardwired it becomes, defining you and the world around you.

Your belief system lives in your unconscious mind and shows up unexpectedly. Let's look at a very simple example. Do you squeeze the toothpaste from the bottom or the top? I had a client who was practically in a rage when her husband squeezed the toothpaste in the middle. She repeatedly told him to squeeze it from the bottom. He was well intentioned and wanted to please his wife but could not understand why this was important. He forgot to squeeze the toothpaste in the way his wife wanted him to. As a result, a major fight broke out that almost ended their relationship. She lashed out with everything from, "You do not love me," to, "You don't respect me," to, "You never do anything I ask."

As you can imagine, her husband was in shock. He could not understand how a tube of toothpaste could cause this type of reaction. He began to question his decision to marry his wife and detached from her. Fortunately, his wife and I were able to uncover the source of her reaction in a couple's session, and they were able to make amends.

As it turns out, the wife was severely criticized growing up, from squeezing the toothpaste to doing dishes and everything in between. Her father said to her the very things she threw up to her husband. This unfinished business was waiting for an opportunity to get resolved.

Despite the wife's accomplishments, she still had these experiences stored away in her unconscious. This client used her perfectionism to achieve more, with the hopes she might avoid the anxiety she felt from not measuring up.

Self-awareness is your control switch that enables you to evaluate how relevant your beliefs are and whether you want them to define you and how. Acknowledging feelings goes a long way in resolving them.

Power of Optimism

Distraction and the stress that comes from it sets up negative, cynical, and limited thoughts. Once the negativity starts, it takes more effort to turn those limiting thoughts into positive ones. The quality of your life and your ability to focus is better if you maintain a positive outlook. It is also easier to be positive when you have goals for your day and, ultimately, your life. In turn, the more positive you are, the easier it is to stay focused!

Maintaining a positive attitude is sometimes confused with being a "Pollyanna." Optimism doesn't mean you overlook challenges or ignore potential problems and think only of the good. Optimism is a combination of a hopeful attitude along with the ability to judge the situation realistically. This hopeful attitude is the result of believing in your own skills and abilities and recalling other times you were successful in overcoming challenge like this.

Optimists and pessimists fall along a continuum in these three dimensions:

Permanence: Seeing things as temporary or permanent

> P: *Times are tough. Why bother looking?*
>
> O: *Times are tough. I know it will be hard to find a job, but I have a lot of skills people want.*

Pervasiveness: Seeing things as situational or universal

> P: *Our department restructured, and now I have to work night shift. Managers are all the same. They do not care about people.*
>
> O: *Our department restructured because of the new regulations. I am working night shift, and as soon as the dust settles, I am going to transfer to a new department.*

Personalization: Taking the blame for what happens

> P: *If I would have been on time and showed up at all the meetings, I would not have been put on nights.*
>
> O: *The new regulations have changed how we work, and the department needed my skills on nights.*

As you become more aware, notice what end of the continuum you are on and what might trigger your attitude.

Your Internal GPS: Manage Expectations. Set Boundaries.

Most of us use the GPS on our phone to get around and avoid traffic and accidents. We also have an internal GPS (guide to personal success) that can help us avoid delays in our everyday life, if we tune in to it. This program has been peeling back the layers that keep you from tuning into your inner voice. This chapter is going to touch on two issues that help you stay on course, manage expectations and learn to set boundaries.

Here's an example of how managing your expectations can save your frustration and protect relationships.

Kerrie volunteered to plan her sister in law's baby shower. She wanted to get closer to Jess and thought this would be the perfect way to spend more time together. Kerrie expected they would become more like friends. Excited about the big day, she picked out the color scheme she knew Jess would like, the music, the food and favors, and had carefully selected invitations. They were getting together for dinner to go over the details. Excited to share her great news, she bubbled over with this information as soon as Jess showed up for dinner. When Jess did not appear the least bit excited, or happy about the event, Kerrie shut down and became sullen.

Kerrie said: "I expected to get some appreciation for my effort and 0 wanted Jess to think I was being a great sister in law." In her anticipation of Jess's response, she failed to check in and find out how Jess was doing. Earlier in the week Jess had gotten some disturbing news and wanted to just talk about that before planning the shower. Kerrie was caught up in her world and did not notice Jess's tension.

They both left the dinner further apart than they were before this incident; both disappointed and less trusting of each other.

Expectations of others are a little like perfectionism, they set up barriers to trust, and put unnecessary pressure on the other person. Expecting the best will happen is a great mindset to have. Expecting other people will respond in the way you want them to, is a barrier to success.

The above is a personal example of NOT managing expectations with your close relationships. At work it is equally important to manage expectations with your boss, other departments and customers if you are a business owner. If you want to have successful relationships and get it done at work, you will need to master expectations. And I have a formula to help you do just that.

To manage expectations means you influence someone's belief about what they expect to happen. In the case of business, your product solves a problem, and your marketing influences a sale. You have success.

Unfortunately, it doesn't work that smoothly most of the time. There are many unknowns. You need a strategy.

Expectations are influenced by what you believe, the past, the desire or passion associated with it, assumptions, pressures, other people, external messaging, work related goals and priorities. It is our responsibility to manage those expectations to have healthy and fulfilling relationships, success at work, and less stress along the way.

As noted in the example, expectations can create drama and increase the stress reaction, if they are not managed.

Let's start with managing your expectations. We have talked about self-awareness throughout this program, this is a critical element to owning your power and having success. Here are the steps to manage your expectations:

Step 1: Know what you want. Be honest with you.

Whether it is personal or professional, know your desired outcome, make sure it is measurable, so you know when you have achieved it.

Step 2: Do not make assumptions.

Managing expectations is challenging with people you do not know, and sometimes, even harder with those you know. You assume you know what they want and like. Open your mind, be aware of the potential biases you might have, to avoid assumptions.

Step 3: Listen, ask, understand.

Take the time to ask questions, listen, and ask more questions in order to understand what the other person wants. What are their expectations? This is true for people you do not know well and those you do.

Step 4: Be present to what is going on within you, and around you.

Mindfulness helps you avoid emotional hijacking or being caught off guard by emotional reactions, yours or someone else's. It will also help you get in touch with what you really want.

It is natural to have expectations for your life; the problem comes when you insist other people meet those expectations. Make the time to build a foundation in the relationship that allows you both to negotiate these expectations.

Managing Other's Expectations

If you are a business owner, you want to meet and exceed your customer's expectations, to stand out in the marketplace. As an employee you want to manage expectations of your boss, so you do not get overloaded with work, and continue to perform at high standards. The same is true in personal situations, it is important to manage what other people expect of you, so you can build trust and deepen intimacy.

Successful expectation management requires you are consistent in meeting your goals and satisfying those people who are invested in your performance. When your performance becomes dependable, everyone can get on the same page.

Here are guidelines to help you manage other people's expectations.

1. Communicate. Communicate. Communicate.

Too often plans fail or expectations are not met because there was not enough communication in the planning stage about what is important, when and how it gets delivered.

Since no two people receive messages in the same way, you want to clarify that what people heard, is what you said, and meant. Avoid confusing and conflicting messages; be direct.

And if you are unsure. Ask. You can always follow up your conversation with, "Did that make sense to you? Let's confirm what is being agreed upon."

2. Anticipate what other people may want.

This is not trying to read their mind. By asking questions, clarifying their answer, you can help the other person identify their needs, and you will be able to anticipate what might work for them. Very often, someone may want something for you but are not clear on the deliverables. Help them figure it out by asking questions.

This is very helpful in work-related situations. Being able to solve your customers' (or bosses') problems makes you indispensable.

This is also true for personal situations, ask questions, use examples, clarify and understand what is expected.

3. Design your feedback loop.

How will you handle communication flow, feedback, boundaries for your workload, uncertainty, mix ups?

Successful interventions are designed within a system that includes the types of interaction, modes of communication needed, and what happens when there are conflicts, or a need for revision.

I use an agile lean framework that will make the process visual. I will incorporate Kanban boards, a variety of meeting and report formulas to discuss progress and gain agreement on the timeline. This can also be applied to personal situations!

When you have a personal situation, it pays to go through this level of planning; it will save you distress overall. In planning the shower, Kerrie would have been better served to ask Jess how she preferred to be updated; does she want text messages, photos sent, email or something else?

She could use a project planning tools that includes a calendar with timelines, tasks and accountability. This can be communicated in the preferred format: text, email, or through a virtual connection on a laptop.

By working out a system to deal with the various details of the event, their relationship could have been preserved and their time together spent sharing more about what was happening with each other.

Boundaries: Where do you begin and end?

"I try so hard to be nice. I have listened to her problems for twenty years, and nothing changes. I make time for my mother any time she calls, and she is still lonely. What am I doing wrong?"

—Lucy

5:30 a.m.

The alarm goes off. Still tired from too little sleep, Lucy dreads the day. She agreed to come into work on her day off to help the Charge Nurse. She remembers the conversation.

"Lucy, we have a staffing crunch with Monika sick and two people on vacation, and I need someone for day shift tomorrow. You are always so dependable; I just knew you would get us out of this problem. Can you work Tuesday? I know it is your day off, but we really need you."

While Lucy agrees, she knows she was supposed to fix brownies for her daughter's play and sew her costume on Tuesday. Deep down inside, she is aware of feeling good that she is needed.

As Lucy gets in the shower, she thinks about the visit with her good friend, Teresa, who stopped by last evening unannounced. Teresa is going through a breakup, and she needed to talk. Lucy offered her wine and made her a light dinner because Teresa had said she had not eaten. Lucy pushed aside the nagging resentment that comes up when Teresa shows up. It is a one-sided relationship. After all, she needs me, Lucy told herself. Teresa knew Lucy was working today and stayed late anyway. She told Lucy, "I just need someone to talk to." In the back of Lucy's mind, she remembers being there for Teresa at every one of her five breakups in the last year. But who's counting? Lucy told herself.

6:00 a.m.

Lucy continues to ruminate about her mother's phone call last week when she started another guilt trip. "Lucy, you never bring the girls by anymore. Don't you love your mother?" Lucy starts to get angry and then quickly reminds herself that it must be tough living alone since her mother lost her husband. Though, her parents divorced when Lucy was eight, and her mother lived alone for over twenty years and did fine. Lucy dismisses that thought.

Lucy makes her daughters' lunches and, in the process, quickly eats three cookies and half of a sandwich, without even realizing it. She thinks to herself: "One of these days, I have to sit down and eat. I know this is why I can't lose weight. I hate being fat."

Ignoring the sadness that wells up, remembering herself just a year ago at her ideal weight, she moves on, grabs her coffee, and shouts to her husband, "I am leaving! Lunches are on the counter, and the girls have to be at school by 7:30."

6:30 a.m.

In the car, Lucy thinks about the day and remembers she is working with Pat. Pat is someone Lucy has admired because she is able to say no and stand up for herself. Pat went through a divorce and, as a result, went to counseling. Pat told her it was the best thing that happened to her because she learned to tune in to herself and recognize she needed to take care of herself in order to take care of other people. Lucy was thinking: "Pat was always talking about boundaries. I have no idea what Pat means. What are boundaries?"

Can you relate to Lucy? Do you try hard to "be nice" while you compromise your own interests? As mentioned in the previous section, anger's message is to set limits and boundaries. You must be aware of what you are feeling in order to take action. Lucy lives in tune with everyone else's needs and ignores her own. She tries hard to be helpful, and yet, her life just isn't working. She is overweight, in emotional pain, and ends up feeling like she failed even after all her efforts. Lucy is spending all her energy fixing other people's problems, pleasing everyone but herself, and being nice out of fear she will upset someone.

Setting boundaries can be a tough lesson, especially if the following questions are running in the background:

1. Can I set limits and still be a nice person?

2. What if my limits make it hard on someone else?

3. Is it selfish to set limits?

4. If I am supposed to set limits, why do I feel so guilty?

Boundaries are easy to spot in the physical world: people put up fences, close the door, pull down the shades, and define their own spaces. Your body uses its proprioceptive system to note its position in space, and you move through your environment as a result of this system. This is the equivalent of your aura and extends out an arm's length around your body. Different cultures have different limits when it comes to personal space.

It is harder to set the intangible emotional and spiritual boundaries. This is especially challenging when you are not tuned in to your emotions. Boundaries define what is you and not you. Boundaries define what you are responsible for and what you are not responsible for. This gives you freedom to know exactly what you must take care of and what is someone else's responsibility. You are not responsible for other people, even when they try to manipulate or guilt you into believing you are. The guilt and manipulation work because you are out of touch with your own feelings and your emotional GPS (guide to personal success).

Let's answer the above questions about limits. Contrary to what most people believe, setting limits makes you a nice person, as you are take care of yourself, you give others permission to do the same. When you fall into the trap of being manipulated (or manipulating) you take over others' responsibility for themselves, you are depriving them of the opportunity to grow.

Second, your boundaries are all about you and no one else. If someone complains about your limits, it is their issue. They may be trying to manipulate or guilt you into doing what they want you to do.

Third, it is not selfish to set limits when your internal GPS is sending out signals (anger) to take some type of action. To be caring and loving to others means you are responsible to them and not for them; helping someone with something they cannot do for themselves is different than being responsible for someone and doing things they can do for themselves. If you constantly say yes to various demands from others, the person asking is not going to look for alternative ways to get their needs met.

> **Boundaries are how you take care of you and encourage others to take care of themselves.**

Just like a fence that has a gate, boundaries are meant to open and close. Boundaries are not a rigid structure like a wall, just as they are not made of sand and permeable to any pressure. It takes practice to set boundaries.

Boundaries are also about what you allow into your life as much as they are about what you limit in your life. Are you so tuned in to others you cannot give yourself the time and energy to tend to your interests and needs?

Learning to say yes in your life is also part of boundaries. What have you been denying yourself because it is so hard to say yes?

Begin with awareness of your feelings. They will let you know when someone is crossing the line. Remember, Lucy was resentful and felt sad when she remembered her ideal weight. Sadness is about letting go of something that is not working anyway. Being all things to all people was not working in Lucy's life. Making the decision to take care of herself and lose weight could be a turning point for Lucy as she lets go of this focus on what other people need and tune in to what she needs.

Ways You Can Set Boundaries

Words are ways you set limits. Saying no lets people know your limits. You have to say no more in order to say yes to things you want in your life.

Susan has trouble saying no. Her whole life was falling apart because of it. Susan's husband injured his back and was out of work. To be able to help him, she went on night shift. Susan was working on a promotion and going off dayshift could interfere with her chances. The management team wanted to evaluate her for the position. They understood she wanted to take care of her husband and agreed to give her six weeks before making the final decision.

Susan helped her husband through the surgery and the recovery and saw him making progress. He was walking and able to take care of himself. Susan wanted to tell her husband she was going back on dayshift to go for the promotion but knew he would be angry.

Thinking about the situation, Susan got angry also, this was the motivation she needed to finally stand up for herself. She ruminated: "How could he expect me to give up even more after all I have done for him?" Susan knew to stay on nights and continue to take care of her husband would mean she would lose out on the promotion. She kept thinking, "who knows when another chance will come around?"

As a nurse, she knew he was well enough to take care of himself. As his wife, her eyes were opened, and she recognized he was enjoying all the special attention. For so long, she had enabled him to take advantage of her, by taking responsibility for his well-being. She finally realized she could set boundaries and take care of herself.

Consequences to Setting Boundaries

Some people put up "No Trespassing" signs to ensure other people stay off their property. There can be legal consequences if you trespass.

What are the consequences if someone trespasses on your emotional boundaries? It is important to stick to your guns when you set limits. For example, if a friend is always late, you might very firmly say, "Next time you are late, please call me so I can make other arrangements." It can also be a simple request, "When we go out, I prefer to drive."

Setting boundaries is much more fluid when you are in touch with your emotions and listen to their guidance. Trusting your intuition, respecting your anger, and learning to relax so you can tune in will help you set and hold your boundaries. Being able to define where you stop and someone else begins keeps you from taking on someone else's emotions.

Anger and shame can help you set a boundary that is neither too far out nor too limiting. Fear, anxiety, and worry can keep your boundary so tight around you that it restricts your life. As you learn to ground yourself, relax, and become more present to your emotions and feelings, setting boundaries becomes more natural.

Boundary Check-in

Separating yourself from difficult or hurtful situations (or people) is necessary to get perspective and get in touch with yourself. You do not need stay in potentially abusive situations. Leaving the room or moving out of town are examples of physical distance, just as taking time off from relationships that are causing pain will be a way to gain a new perspective as you protect yourself.

Use the following self-check to evaluate your boundary setting. Rate yourself on the following statements using the "1-to-10" scale, one being never and ten being always.

1. It is hard for me to decide.

2. It is hard to look people in the eye.

3. It is hard to take care of myself.

4. I take care of others and have little left for myself.

5. I am embarrassed and feel different from other people.

6. I do not spend time alone.

7. I cannot keep secrets.

The higher the score, the more difficulty you have in setting boundaries.

Question 1 speaks to the intrusion of other people's beliefs, thoughts, and feelings into their own and the difficulty in knowing what they really prefer.

Question 2 is about feeing bad about who you are, worried others can see right through you. When you have healthy boundaries and feel good about yourself, you can look people in the eye and not worry about getting lost or being seen for who you are. Do you struggle with the Imposter Syndrome?

Questions 3 and 4 are about other people taking up so much space in your own emotional space, there is no room for your own needs. You now find your sense of accomplishment through caretaking others.

Question 5 speaks to the loss of boundaries in defining who you are. When one becomes enmeshed with others, your own uniqueness can feel wrong or bad.

Question 6 speaks to being out of touch with yourself and your inner-life. When you are spending your time and energy looking outside of yourself, it is the equivalent of rejecting yourself. When you do finally spend time alone, you may be overwhelmed with critical self-talk and emotions.

Question 7 relates to an all-or-nothing approach to communicating what is going on. You may have had early messaging about not telling anyone anything about what you feel and experienced toxic secrets in your life, so telling everything is your way to balance.

Setting and maintaining boundaries becomes easier as you learn to acknowledge your emotions and listen to their wisdom.

The Past: The Number-One Barrier to Future Success

I worked with a highly successful financial analyst who we can call Jon. He spent years working on large deals and achieving high levels of success, both financially and professionally. When he made the decision to change his lifestyle and follow his passion for photography, he thought he would finally have the peace he was seeking. Instead, he felt stuck and afraid.

Jon described it this way: "I do not see how I could *ever* achieve the level of success I have had in the financial world. I am starting out behind and can never catch up." Even though it was his decision to leave the world of financial deals, he was measuring his future against his past. The way he saw it, he was starting out as a failure.

Regardless of your level of success, how you think about your past is the number-one barrier to future success. This is true for individuals and organizations. The last success becomes a barrier to the next because of the self-talk that drives your actions.

In this chapter, we will explore how you think about yourself, your belief system, and other mindset distortions that drown your creativity and stifle your future.

You may be thinking, *I've had a rotten past. Surely I'm justified in thinking, "If it weren't for my past..."* No, regardless of your past—even if it was filled with difficulty, trauma, and challenges—you cannot use your past to procrastinate over your future.

Deal with your past, and let it go.

We will be talking about distortions in your thinking in this chapter. There is a natural tendency to underestimate the effort required to show up at your best and to overestimate how you showed up in your past.

Internal Conflict: When Your Future Self Procrastinates

Cognitive dissonance is when your belief system runs counter to your behavior. One of my clients, who we will call Geralyn, struggled with fears and self-doubt, yet still achieved remarkable success in her career. She hit the wall as she came up to her next promotion and could not see how she would *ever* go beyond where she was now.

Then there was John, who began his business as a carpenter. He was excellent at what he did and found himself building houses and then renovating commercial spaces. He came to me when he hit his wall. He had a multimillion-dollar business and still saw himself as a carpenter. He was losing money on bids and hesitated to bid on larger projects. He was stuck.

These are just two examples out of the many clients I've worked with to help them go beyond where they were.

This internal conflict is draining! Not only is your brain out of sync, but so are other systems in your body, mind, and spirit. How far can you go when you are fighting against yourself?

Check in: How often do you experience the following?

Signs of Dissonance

Are you experiencing?	Frequency: Daily, Weekly, Monthly
Disorganized, cluttered spaces	
Moodiness	
Anxiety	
No confidence	
Procrastination	
Can't concentrate	
Confused about what is next	
Catastrophic thinking	
No inner harmony	

Going through the analysis in Chapter 2 will help you align your values, goals, and dreams, which decreases your dissonance. Chapter 1 teaches you tools that will build your coherence.

Check in: Look at the chart below. How often are you in sync?

Signs of Coherence

Are you experiencing?	Frequency: Daily, weekly, Monthly
Top performance	
Happiness, joy (most of the time)	
Feeling calm	
Confidence	
Acting on goals	
Focus, ability to concentrate	
Organized	
Feeling of certainty	
Overall wellbeing	

Do you feel stuck?

Tune in to yourself and write out your self-talk around moving forward.

_____

_____

_____

_____

_____

Procrastination

Procrastination is something we have all done. Sometimes, procrastination is a way to deal with delays from other people and it is how you choose to cope. And then there is procrastination that can have severe and costly consequences.

Mirabelle came to me because she had procrastinated paying her taxes and was facing severe penalties. "I felt so overwhelmed with my business and my husband's business. I was responsible for the paperwork. I did not realize how much this drained my energy and it was something I continued to put off."

In the next section, you will learn about cognitive biases that may explain why people procrastinate.

There is a natural tendency to overestimate your own ability and underestimate how much time and resources are required, so some people may find they have more to do in the last minute than they can handle.

Procrastination can lead to more serious mental health issues as the pressure and stress to finish tasks at the last-minute mounts. Some of the reasons people procrastinate include:

- Lack of clarity around what they need to do
- Not having the ability to do the job
- Lack of focus
- Habit of waiting
- Feeling like you must be "in the right mood" to accomplish the task

Using procrastination is one-way perfectionists manage their anxiety around needing to be perfect.

The important thing is to be aware of *why* you are procrastinating to give you control over the outcome. Is there performance anxiety and fear, or are you overloaded with work?

One of the tools I like to use to get things done and keep my workflow from getting out of hand is a Kanban Board. Check out the video online on using Kanban.

Bias: Mindset Distortion

Most of us think of ourselves as rational and capable of making good decisions. Yet the difference between a good decision and one that isn't could be a bias. How often do you evaluate whether your decisions are good and bias-free?

There are over 100 biases listed in Wikipedia—over 100 ways we can distort information. Through observation or interaction, we take information in and process it through our filters, which include fears and bias, both falling under the radar of consciousness. As you make decisions (or choose not to make them), how do you know you are not distorting information with an expectation bias, or a distortion bias, or a status quo bias (and the list goes on)?

Bias will steer our thoughts and decisions in subtle ways: we may end up being more optimistic than realistic, fall prey to a confirmation bias, or get caught up in a fear scenario that has little probability of happening but feels scary in the moment.

Consider these different types of biases.

Blind Spot Bias

This is when you deny your own biases. In other words, "everyone else is biased, and I am not. I am too intelligent, smart, savvy . . ." (You name it.) The truth is, we are all potentially guilty of all these biases. Acknowledgement is the first step to overcoming them.

Confirmation Bias

This is what leads you to look for evidence to support what you already know. You view the facts as either confirmation of what you know, or you discount any facts that do not support your view.

Anchoring Effect

This is the tendency to rely on the initial piece of evidence you encounter. This is what happens in negotiation: the initial number presented anchors in the bidding going forward.

Optimism Bias

This leads one to underestimate projects, overlooking potential pitfalls and skewing costs or duration.

Availability Bias

This skews perception of events based on the emotional availability in our memory. For example, one may think traveling by plane is more dangerous that traveling by car due to the dramatic imagery of a plane crash.

Estimation Bias (called Fundamental Attribution Error)

This is when you overestimate someone's weakness (internal characteristics) and underestimate circumstances. Have you ever accused someone of being disrespectful because they kept you waiting, only to have to explain why you were late yourself? The tendency is to underestimate the influence of our internal characteristics and overestimate circumstances.

Dave frequently criticized his coworker, Sara, for coming in late. They both had children, but Dave prided himself on keeping to a schedule. "Sara, you need to have a plan and to stick to it." When Dave ended up being late, he blamed the extra heavy morning commute for why he did not make it on time, when in fact, he had overslept. He did not want to admit he could be guilty of overlooking such an important element of work.

This bias happens all the time and is the source of conflict, misunderstanding, and a breakdown in communication. The fact is, we routinely ignore situational influences and frequently rush to judgement about someone.

With this bias, when you find yourself peeved by someone else's behavior, take a moment and identify two to four positive characteristics of that person. It will help you balance your opinion. You may also increase your awareness of your own behavior relative to what upset you in someone else.

Research has found that because of the unconscious influence and the amount of information it takes in, "reality" is not perceived directly compared to the conscious mind. Much of what you "know" and even observe is filtered through the lens of your early experiences, these biases, and your belief systems. The mind filters everything that happens to us through this lens of our internal mental models.

How can you improve your thinking?

First, realize there is a lot more going on internally than we realize. Reducing pressure and stress allows you to access higher functions of the brain, broaden your perspective, and decrease reactions. Under stress, the brain is hardwired to survive. It takes a deliberate effort to engage your brain to thrive.

Managing emotions and regulating your internal impulses will improve your thinking. Without the reactions getting in the way, you can consider the context of what is happening versus rushing to judgment. Self-awareness and self-regulation are the foundation of emotional intelligence.

Use reflection to evaluate your thinking and your decisions; engage in a systematic problem-solving approach like Lean Sigma. (Lean Sigma is an approach to continuous improvement and problem solving used worldwide.)

Allow yourself to consider that others may be right, more often than you think!

We can't solve problems by using the same kind of thinking we used when we created them.

Albert Einstein

Living Life Deliberately

Albert Einstein not only changed the foundation of scientific thinking when he introduced the theory of relativity ($E=MC^2$), but he also changed the way people think about the world. He acknowledged his genius was the result of both using his analytic brain and infusing it with the flow of creativity to help shape his theories and conclusions. Another of his quotes:

> "Imagination is more important than knowledge."

Right before he wrote about the speed of light, he had a dream of riding on a moonbeam. There are other stories of imagination creating a breakthrough in conventional wisdom. August Kekulé, famous chemist and founder of the theory of chemical structure, discovered the structure of the benzene ring during a daydream when he saw an image of a snake eating its tail. He also saw dancing atoms and molecules and came up with the theory of chemical structure.[4]

These discoveries changed the foundation of science and how people see the world. They came from the integration of both the right and left sides of the brain, a blend of analytic and creative intelligence.

The fact is, our brain naturally thinks in images. This is how we all learned to speak, write, and learn. Visualization is a power tool that integrates your natural instinct to think in images with the rational mind. Before I take you through the steps, let me tell you a story.

In 1940, Alcoa wanted to keep up the demand for their one product, aluminum.[5] They created a program that blended imagination with engineering to come up with innovations. They called it "Imagineering." Today, that word is trademarked by Disney to reflect how they combine imagination with engineering to transform swampland into a remarkable theme park.

> **Your brain naturally thinks in images.**

This blend of imagination and analysis is at the foundation of resilient thinking and the style of visualization I am introducing here. For over twenty years, I've coached thousands of individuals to change the way they think, including breaking free of anxiety, self-doubt, fear, and other destructive patterns of thinking and feeling. To break through the client's resistance and clarify their goal, I used techniques like hypnosis, imagery, and energy clearing to shift their attention and thought patterns. After working with so many people for so long, I learned a lot about changing behavior (and mindset) to achieve success.

Everything we learn, our brain first "sees" as an image. We easily accessed this as children; we were instinctually inclined to use our imagination in play. During school years, this inclination is quickly extinguished in the process of learning. Most people do not notice the loss of this great skill until life throws them a curve ball and forces them into a major transition.

This is when most of my clients seek help: either their business, career, or marriage is falling apart, and they need help making sense of it all. I want to share this tool to help you not just avoid hitting the wall, but to also increase your everyday innovation and creativity. Once you learn this, you can use it in any situation to discover new and effective ways to operate.

Resilient thinking is grounded in this power tool. I will first take you through the process of visualization and then walk you through your analysis. This two-step process of visualization is extremely effective in moving beyond the roadblocks of limiting beliefs or mental models that are outdated or too small.

When you deliberately use the power of visualization, you will increase your opportunity to succeed and achieve the very thing you want – even when it seems out of reach. You will expend less effort by using this approach to lose the worry, fear, or doubt about how things will turn out.

Worry and fear are the negative use of visualization. Stop working against yourself.

Visualization is the intentional use of your mind to achieve success.

Remember what we talked about in the section on Flow? How you use your attention determines your success. Visualization is the deliberate and intentional use of your attention. Use this process to experience the desired outcome before conversations with employees, your boss, or the Board. It is great to use as you plan for your new initiative and see all things working out the way you want them. Using visualization in this way helps you relax while you practice the situation in your mind, going through all the steps as if you were actually doing it.

Golfers, musicians, and all successful people use this power tool to practice and develop skills, increase confidence and muscle memory, and get the results they want.

Chronic stress sets up a fear-based motivation, causing you to spend time imagining worst-case scenarios or engaging in negative, worrisome thoughts and catastrophic thinking. Knowing what we know about the plasticity of the brain, getting stuck in negative, limited thoughts can quickly become your default perspective. Your brain adapts to the thoughts and activities you most often engage, and this becomes your default mode of thinking.

> **How do you direct your attention? Are you focused on what isn't working and feeling gloomy, or are you focused on possibility and feeling energized?**

Beginning a practice of regular visualization of what you want (as opposed to worrying about what you fear might happen) will increase your confidence. With a regular practice of visualization, you enhance skills and strengthen feelings of empowerment. You are also relaxing while you *experience the outcome you really want*. This changes your attitude, approach, and perception of what is happening, which then changes how you come across to others. Relaxed leaders are more creative and effective.

Visualization helps keep your motivation high. It is common and typical for motivation to wax and wane. In the beginning of a new program, motivation is strong, and everything is easy. As the weeks move on, your desires may seem less as stress takes its toll on your enthusiasm. As challenges show up, your resolve to continue to adopt new behaviors may weaken.

You need a "motivation reboot." You have probably experienced this when you have started a new diet or exercise plan or when you decided to change a bad habit. This is also true for any new initiative at work. As the day-to-day tasks grind away at you, it is easy to get bogged down in the details; your goals for starting your new program may be further away in your mind and harder to get excited about.

Whenever you are rolling out a new program at work, keep the results you want in the forefront of your mind. Visualization helps you create a success map.

What do you want to happen? What will your day or life look like as a result of this new program? Define it, and then imagine it. Experience it, feel it, and get as detailed as possible. Hold the expectation. Really feel the achievement of this goal.

Use this tool with all things big and small. Do you have trouble communicating with an employee? See your next conversation flowing smoothly. Do the same with your spouse, children, and friends. Release the struggle of trying too hard and use visualization to see what you want to happen.

Do you want new skills in communication, optimism, resilience, and emotional intelligence? See yourself interacting and succeeding. Just as with mindfulness, when your mind wanders and brings up questions, distracting thoughts, or problems, go back to the image of you handling the problems and seeing everything going your way. This is a good exercise in building confidence. This is a competitive edge you will have as you adopt this power tool.

As life demands more of you, it is easy to give your energy to the urgency right in front of you, leaving yourself frustrated and feeling negative about what is possible. A regular habit of visualization will keep you focused on your goals.

Researchers who criticize the use of visualization, citing decrease in drive as a result of seeing success, acknowledge that the brain reacts "as if" the imagined scenario actually happened.[6]

What the above research demonstrates is that even though visualization doesn't *always* motivate, it does change your brain. In other words, this process is powerful.

Tips to Make Visualization Work for You

1. **Relax**. Give yourself time prior to the visualization to relax. Use deliberate breathing, tell yourself to relax, and imagine yourself letting all the tension drain away.

2. **Have a goal.** What do you want to achieve with this visualization exercise? It does not have to be a lofty goal. It can be simple, but you must start with a specific goal.

3. **Do not get hung up on *how* this will happen**. I want to share a powerful story of how you can use visualization without trying to figure out the details.

    If you play golf, you probably know the name Ben Hogan. Early in his golfing career, he suffered a devastating car accident and was told he would never walk again. He told his wife to bring his golf clubs into the hospital room. The physicians were against it because they did not want him to have "false" hope.

    Ben had conviction and a strong personality, and his desire won out. His clubs sat in the corner for many months, and as he went through his treatment, he would imagine himself playing the game, swinging the clubs, and walking the course. After a year, he did walk again. He went on to win many golf championships.

4. **Bring clarity and accuracy to your vision.** Make your vision clear and focused. As you imagine, experience this as if it were happening in this moment. Visualization engages all the senses.

    Some people do not actually "see" images; rather, they feel the experience or think about it. Use all your senses to make this visualization clear and focused. Ben imagined he was golfing and applied his knowledge of the sport to accurately imagine the experience, using all his senses. Musicians apply the detail of their skill and talent to imagine they are playing the piece flawlessly. Use your skill in the area in which you are imagining by filling in certain details. Allow your body to engage muscle memory when appropriate and make this visualization very real.

5. **Be open**. Refrain from using a good or bad type of judgment as you visualize. This is the power behind mindfulness: your mind learns to relax, so you can simply experience the moment without giving it an emotional charge of being good, bad, right, wrong, difficult, easy, perfect, or not. If you struggle with believing you will achieve the goal, then back your vision down to something you can experience as real.

6. **Stay in the moment**. See the vision as happening right now, not next week or next year. Your unconscious mind does not have the dimension of time, and if you see something happening next year, you will always be a year away from your goal.

7. **Keep this to yourself.** Do not share your visualization with anyone. This is *your* goal, and you do not want someone else's opinion.

A Simple Exercise in Visualization

As a child, you used your imagination easily. You were not filled with doubt about being "realistic" or worried about being playful. You simply used your imagination to relieve stress and learn.

This is a simple exercise using the basic technique of visualization.

1. Think about something you want. Keep it simple and something you can easily see yourself having. It could be an object, event, or a circumstance.

2. Get comfortable. Make sure you won't be disturbed. Give yourself 15 minutes. Use a timer.

3. Starting from the top of your head, move all the way down your body and relax. Release tension. Count down from ten to one and tell yourself to relax even more as you count down.

4. As you relax, imagine what you want happening exactly as you wish it to be. Feel the experience as if it were happening now. See people coming up to you, your friends smiling, and experience the vivid detail of having what you want.

5. Finish your visualization acknowledging this new reality. You can end with, "And, so it is," or conclude with, "I now have (fill in the blank)."

   This is an important part of the visualization. Too often, people end up disbelieving the visualization and going back into the fear or doubt mode. This only creates confusion or ambivalence within you, causing your actions to reflect this.

6. Once you visualize, let it go. Do not think about it. Do this for 15 minutes, every day, for two weeks. Journal throughout the process and note any surprises, coincidences, or resistance that shows up. Be observant and mindful. Refrain from judging.

The Next Step in Visualization

This step will help clarify your goals and create very specific visualizations. You have already done some analysis on your desired goals.

As part of this exercise, chose one of your goals or mile markers. This does not have to be your biggest goal. Choose something to work through this process.

Identify your goal in measurable terms:

I.e., I want to lose 15 lbs., wear a size 6, earn $250,000, or get promoted to Director of the department...

_____

_____

_____

Now, answer the following:

Why not you? List at least three reasons you should not get this goal.

1.

2.

3.

You will use energy clearing on this shortly. If you can list more than three reasons, put them down.

Why not NOW? List three reasons why NOW is not the right time.

1.

2.

3.

You will use energy clearing on these three reasons next. If you can list more than three reasons, put them down

Energy Clearing: Step 2 of Visualization

As you read through the two lists on the previous page, tap or rub on these two points. They are just below your clavicle and outside of your sternal notch.

Read through the list and tap or rub. Allow whatever emotion to flow as it comes up, releasing it with every tap. Spend five minutes going through this process. It is important to keep tapping when you feel the emotions come up.

THIS IS A RELEASE EXERCISE. If you stop tapping when emotions come up, you shut down the release process.

I have a video and explanation of the energy field in the online program.

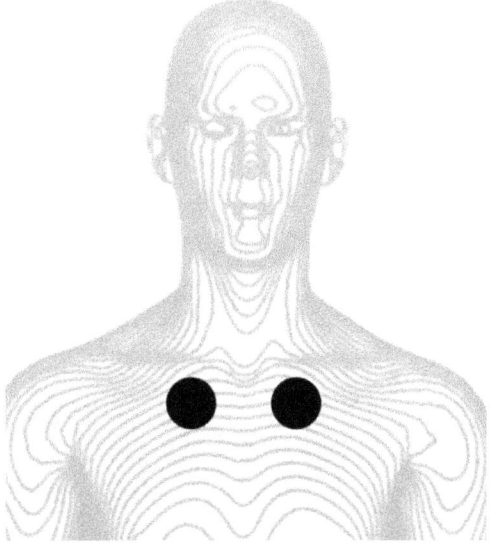

Now that you have cleared your resistance, write out your desired outcome with specific, descriptive words. Experience it as your reality. As you write, imagine the experience in full color and stereo!

Be clear enough that if someone were reading your description, they would immediately understand. Once you write it out, go back and reread it, fully experiencing every detail. Do this every day for at least two weeks.

Describe your ideal life:

Tips for Success

Personal development is an ongoing process. It happens in a spiral fashion rather than along a straight line. Having read this book and gone through the online program, take some time and evaluate the process.

Did you learn something that will change how you go through your day?

This can be one of your measures of success because one day is a microcosm of your life. String together more days with you focused on your main goals, and you will arrive at your destination.

Here is a Tip Checklist to help you apply what you've learned.

Tip Checklist

1. **Do the exercises.** They will awaken your inner genius.

2. **Keep your process quiet.** Much of this reflection is for your eyes only. When you talk about this, share with people you trust to honor you.

3. **Continue to fill in the Big 100 List.** You will be surprised at what you learn when you push yourself to write down things that excite you and bring you joy. You may also identify limiting beliefs you can release!

4. **Keep your Habits Log.** It is so helpful to strengthen new habits.

5. **Use the 100 Day Roadmap.** It takes time to learn how to break down your goals into smaller day-to-day steps. Keep working at it, and you will have a system that will consistently help you achieve results.

Appendix

5 Whys

This simple technique produces powerful results. It originated in the 1930's as part of Toyota's "go and see" philosophy, where managers spent time on the shop floor to get to the root of problems. The technique is still used today.

It is powerful for personal situations as well as problem-solving work-related situations.

This is helpful with simple to moderately difficult problems. And very powerful when you want to get to the root cause of some of your behavior. It is helpful to discover your purpose and the motivation behind what you are doing.

1. Observe the problem in action if possible. Define the problem, write it out.

2. Then ask Why?

Let's say the problem is:

You want to go for that promotion or start that business, but every time you have an opportunity to network, you find an excuse.

To answer the question, you want to think about what is happening and speak to the facts rather than make up potential reasons that this is happening. Let's go with this example:

Why? ▶ ▶ ▶ ▶ I talked myself out of it.

Why? ▶ ▶ ▶ ▶ I do not feel ready to take the leap.

Why? ▶ ▶ ▶ ▶ I was always told I was not good working independently.

Why? ▸ ▸ ▸ ▸ This was my mother's story. She married right out of high school.

Why? ▸ ▸ ▸ ▸ That was typical in that generation.

Review:

What this exercise revealed in this situation is how much of her mother's story, this woman is living out. She became aware of how her mother's opinions and beliefs were still shaping her as an adult.

Solution:

Work on rewriting your story. Change how you talk to you. First, focus on your strengths and write out examples of how they play out in your life.

Descriptions of the Sixty Strengths

*60 Strengths based on the Strengths Profile, developed by Capps	
Action You feel compelled to act immediately and decisively, being keen to learn as you go.	**Curiosity** You are interested in everything, constantly seeking out new information and learning more.
Adaptable You juggle things to meet changing demands and find the best fit for your needs.	**Detail** You naturally focus on the small things that others easily miss, ensuring accuracy.
Adherence You love to follow processes, operating firmly within rules and guidelines.	**Drive** You are very self-motivated, pushing yourself hard to achieve what you want out of life.
Adventure You love to take risks and stretch yourself outside your comfort zone.	**Emotional Awareness** You are acutely aware of the emotions and feelings of others.
Authenticity You are always true to yourself, even in the face of pressure from others.	**Empathic** You feel connected to others through your ability to understand what they are feeling.
Bounceback You use setbacks as springboards to go on and achieve even more.	**Enabler** You create the conditions for people to grow and develop for themselves.
Catalyst You love to motivate and inspire others to make things happen.	**Equality** You ensure that everyone is treated equally, paying close attention to issues of fairness.
Centered You have an inner composure and self-assurance, whatever the situation.	**Esteem Builder** You help others to believe in themselves and see what they are capable of achieving.

Change Agent You are constantly involved with change, advocating for change and making it happen.	**Feedback** You provide fair and accurate feedback to others, to help them develop.
Compassion You really care about others, doing all you can to help and sympathize.	**Gratitude** You are constantly thankful for the positive things in your life.
Competitive You are constantly competing to win, wanting to perform better and be the best.	**Growth** You are always looking for ways to grow and develop, whatever you are doing.
Connector You make connections between people, instinctively making links and introductions.	**Humility** You are happy to stay in the background, giving others credit for your contributions.
Counterpoint You always bring a different viewpoint to others, whatever the situation or context.	**Humor** You see the funny side of almost everything that happens - and make a joke of it.
Courage You overcome your fears and do what you want to do in spite of them.	**Improver** You constantly look for better ways of doing things and how things can be improved.
Creativity You strive to produce work that is original, by creating and combining things in imaginative ways.	**Explainer** You are able to simplify things so that others can understand.

Incubator You love to think deeply about things, to arrive at the best conclusion.	**Prevention** You think ahead, to anticipate and prevent problems before they happen.

Innovation You approach things in ingenious ways, coming up with new and different approaches.	**Pride** You strive to produce work that is of the highest standard and quality.
Judgement You enjoy making decisions and are able to make the right decision quickly and easily.	**Rapport Builder** You establish rapport and relationships with others quickly and easily.
Legacy You want to create things that will outlast you, delivering a positive and sustainable impact.	**Relationship Deepener** You have a natural ability to form deep, long-lasting relationships with people.
Listener You are able to listen intently to and focus on what people say.	**Resilience** You take hardships in your stride, recovering quickly and getting on with things again.
Mission You pursue things that give you a sense of meaning and purpose in your life.	**Resolver** You love to solve problems, the more difficult the better.
Moral Compass You have a strong ethical code, always acting in accordance with what you believe is right.	**Self-awareness** You know yourself well, understanding your own emotions and behavior.
Narrator You love to tell stories and see the power of these stories to convey insights.	**Self-belief** You are confident in your own abilities, knowing that you can achieve your goals.

Optimism You always maintain a positive attitude and outlook on life.	**Service** You are constantly looking for ways to help and serve others.
Organizer You are exceptionally well-organized in everything you do.	**Spotlight** You love to be the focus of everyone's attention.
Persistence You achieve success by keeping going, particularly when things are difficult.	**Strategic Awareness** You pay attention to the wider context and bigger picture to inform your decisions.
Personal Responsibility You take ownership of your decisions and hold yourself accountable for your promises.	**Time Optimizer** You maximize your time, to get the most out of whatever time you have available.
Personalization You recognize everyone as a unique individual, noticing their subtle differences.	**Unconditionality** You accept people for who and what they are, without ever judging them.
Persuasion You enjoy bringing others round to your way of thinking and winning their agreement.	**Work Ethic** You are very hard working, putting a lot of effort into everything you do.
Planner You make plans for everything you do, covering all eventualities.	**Writer** You love to write, conveying your thoughts and ideas through the written word.

Message from Dr. Howard

Dear Reader,

To get the most from this program, do the reflection exercises! It is amazing how quickly things can change when you shine a light on it!

If you feel this book provided value to you, it would mean a lot to me and others **if you would leave a + review on Amazon**.

You can comment on:

1. What you liked most about the book.

2. What was your biggest take away.

And any other comments that would be helpful for other readers. Reviews are so important for authors and I would be very grateful for even a short review.

Stay energized!

Dr. Cynthia Howard

I would love to see you in the membership! I know how much is possible for you having been a part of so many breakthroughs!

www.6keystounstoppable.com

You are not helping anyone when you are stuck.
Step up. Stand out.

What's Stopping You Today Online Membership

This virtual coaching program includes premium online resources to break down self-doubt and help you define your ideal life.

Included in the program:

- Online access 24/7 to premium resources.
- 5 modules, audio, video, checklists, self-assessments ($695 value)
- Strengths Assessment highlighting your top strengths. ($99 value)
- Private FB group with weekly topics, live video with Dr. Howard ($1200 value)
- Monthly live coaching call via zoom ($2400 value)
- Membership in the Work Smart Club with access to premium online training ($295 value)
- Support network to motivate and inspire (priceless)

Visit www.6keystounstoppable.com to register for the program.

To access the program, visit: www.worksmart.club

The Work Smart Club

The Work Smart Club is our online Work and Well-being Center with resources to help you live and work smart. We have short on-the-go training along with courses, templates, guidebooks on subjects you do not normally find elsewhere: managing your energy, developing confidence, strengthening emotional intelligence, handling conflict, identifying strengths, visualization, problem solving, showing up with a bold presence, and so much more.

We want you to be successful at work and in your business. Whether you want to go for that promotion, or develop healthier habits, we have you covered.

We offer a library of premium resources with video, audio, templates, checklists, guidebooks and a monthly live coaching call.

Visit www.worksmart.club.

The program in this book is offered as a course on the Work Smart Club. To log-in to your membership, visit www.worksmart.club/log-in.

About the Author

Cynthia Howard RN, CNC, PhD is an Executive Coach and Performance Expert who helps professionals, leaders, and executives master their mindset and their attention for consistent success.

Cynthia is a mentor, coach, and resilience champion, and in the past twenty-plus years, she has coached thousands of individuals to consistently perform at a high level for greater success and fulfillment.

Dr. Cynthia integrates the latest research in the fields of performance, resilience, and emotional intelligence with the tools in Agile, Lean, Sigma transformation. This combination offers rapid, lasting change.

To contact Cynthia about this program, speaking at your organization, or for a consultation to power up your performance, call toll-free at 1-888-71-FOCUS or email drh@eileadership.org.

www.eileadership.org

Other Books Written by Dr. Howard

The Resilient Leader Mindset Makeover

Energize Your Leadership. Let's talk about the elephant in the room.

Everyday Emotional Intelligence

A Guide to Better Communication. Learn to Handle Fatal Emotions, Drama, Conflict, Bullying.

Resilience: Your Super Power

A Practical Guide for High Performance Leadership

HEAL: Healthy Emotions. Abundant Life.

From Superhero to Super Self-Empowered. Master your Emotional Intelligence.

Endnotes

¹ U.S. Congress Office of Technology Assessment (1991). "Biological Rhythms: Implications for the Worker."

² Dweck, C. (2008) *Mindset: The New Psychology of Success*. Random house: New York.

³ Lipton, B. *The Biology of Belief.*

⁴ Read, J. 1957). *From Alchemy to Chemistry.* pp. 179–180.

⁵ Bykon, M. "Aluminum Exhibits Its Versatility in Art, Life". *JOM* 52 (11) (2000), pp. 9–12.

⁶ Kappesa, H., Oettingena, G. "Positive fantasies about idealized futures sap energy." *Journal of Experimental Social Psychology*, Vol 47, Issue 4. July 2011, 719–729.

⁷ Linley, A. (2008) Average to A+: Realizing Strengths in Yourself and Others, by Alex Linley, CAPP Press.

⁸ World's Most Popular Strengths: Summary Insights from Across the Globe 2018. Whitepaper by Capp & Co., Ltd

⁹ Smith, M. M., Sherry, S. B., Vidovic, V., Saklofske, D. H., Stoeber, J., & Benoit, A. (2019). Perfectionism and the Five-Factor Model of Personality: A Meta-Analytic Review. Personality and Social Psychology Review.

References

Babcock, L. "Nice Girls Don't Ask," Harvard Business Review, 2013.

Babcock, L., Laschever, S. (2007). Women Don't Ask: The High Cost of Avoiding Negotiation—and Positive Strategies for Change. Bantam Books.

Biswas-Diener, R. Kashdan, T. & Minhas, G. A dynamic approach to psychological strength development and intervention, The Journal of Positive Psychology, 6:2, 2011, 106-118

Carr, N. (2011) The Shallows: What the Internet Is Doing to Our Brains. W.W. Norton.

Checkland, P. (1981). Systems Thinking, Systems Practice, Wiley.

Csikszentmihalyi, M. (1990) Flow: The Psychology of Optimal Experience. Harper Perennial: New York.

Goleman, Daniel. (1995). *Emotional intelligence: Why it matters more than IQ.* New York, NY: Bantam Dell.

Howard, Cynthia. (2015) HEAL: Healthy Emotions. Abundant Life. From Super Hero to Super Self Empowered. Santa Maria, CA: Vibrant Radiant Health.

Lazar, S, Kerr, C., Wasserman, R., Gray, J., Greve, D., Treadway, D., McGarvey, M., Quinn, B., Dusek, J., Benson, H., Rauch, S., Moore, C., Fisch, B. "Meditation experience is associated with increased cortical thickness." *Neuroreport*, Vol 16 No 17, 28 Nov 2005. Lippincott, Williams & Wilkins. <http://www.nmr.mgh.harvard.edu/~lazar/Articles/Lazar_Meditation_Plasticity_05.pdf>.

Marks, G., Gudith, D., Klocke, U. "The cost of interrupted work: More speed and stress." University of California, Irvine. <https://www.ics.uci.edu/~gmark/chi08-mark.pdf>

Pyzdek, T., Keller, P., *Six Sigma Handbook.* 2014. McGraw Hill.

Quinlan, D., Swain, N. & Vella-Brodrick, D.A. J Happiness Stud (2012) 13: 1145

Nohria, N. Beer, M. "Cracking the Code of Change" *Harvard Business Review* May June 2000.

Rozin, P., & Royzman, E. "Negativity bias, negativity dominance, and contagion." *Personality and Social Psychology Review,* 5, 2001 296–320.

Wong, C., Law, K. "The effects of leader and follower emotional intelligence on performance and attitude: An exploratory study." The Leadership Quarterly, Volume 13, Issue 3, June 2002, Pages 243–274.

Yeager, D. & Dweck, C. (2012) Mindsets That Promote Resilience: When Students Believe That Personal Characteristics Can Be Developed, Educational Psychologist, 47:4, 302-314,